THE WEIGHT IS OVER

ALEXIS SPIGHT

This book is dedicated to my mother, **Michelle**, who inspired my authorship with the start of her book *"**Cracks in the Pews.**"*

Mom, always remember that you have the power not just to start—but also to finish.

ACKNOWLEDGEMENTS

I would like to express my heartfelt appreciation to the following individuals and ministries whose lives, leadership, inspiration, or support have deeply impacted my journey:

Bishop Mark Tolbert, Bishop Talbert Swan, Pastor Ruby Holland, Pastor Charles Jenkins, Mona McBride, Mona Lisa Sharp, Pastor Craig Pridgen, Kevin Fredricks (KevOnStage), Terry Carr, Moving Forward Fellowship Church (Jacksonville, FL), Lady Pamela Hennings, TyDaye, Tamela Mann, Robert E. Dean, Dr. Derrick and Evangelist Christine King, Prentiss Spight Jr., Le'Andria Johnson, Bishop Brister(Beacon Light International), Bishop Aikens(Memorial Baptist Church), Pastor Nathan and Angel Jackson, Nathan Greene, Pastors Travis and Jackie Green, Pastor CeeJay, Bishop Luther McKinstry, Bishop Dale Bronner, Uncle Jack and Aunt Liz, Jamar Jones, Prentiss Spight Sr., Bishop Joseph Walker, Barbara Callaway, Bishop Randy Borders, and Pastor Marica Chisholm.

TABLE OF CONTENTS

FOREWORD 4
INTRODUCTION 6
CHAPTER 1: 8
CHAPTER 2: 26
CHAPTER 3: 41
CHAPTER 4: 58
CHAPTER 5: 68
CHAPTER 6: 79
CHAPTER 7: 89
CHAPTER 8: 97
CHAPTER 9: 102
CHAPTER 10: 110
CHAPTER 11: 115
CHAPTER 12: 131

FOREWORD

There are moments in ministry when you witness a life that doesn't just speak truth; it lives it, bleeds it, sings it, and dares others to be transformed by it. Alexis Spight is one of those lives. She is not simply a voice in the world; she is a force. A Firestarter. A vessel through whom God continues to pour power, passion, and purpose.

The Weight is Over is not a book you merely read; it's a journey you walk through. And if you're bold enough to take each step with her, you will emerge lighter, stronger, and clearer about who God has called you to be. Alexis holds nothing back. She speaks with the vulnerability of a soul that has wrestled deeply and worshipped harder. This book is drenched in scripture, scarred by life, and saturated in grace.

I've had the distinct honor of watching Alexis grow, not just in gifting, but in godly grit. She has endured private pain in the glare of public platforms and still chooses to lead with love and tell the truth, even when it costs her comfort. That, my friend, is the mark of someone truly called. Her journey isn't polished—it's prophetic. Her insight isn't scripted; it's Spirit-breathed.

In these pages, you'll find healing, laughter, hard truths, and above all, hope. You'll be reminded that discipline is deliverance, that pain has purpose, and that when God gives the signal, it's time to release what was and embrace what is to come.

As her pastor and friend, I couldn't be prouder of her. This book is a gift to the body of Christ and a blueprint for anyone ready to shed the unnecessary and walk fully into destiny.

The wait is over. The weight is over. Now, let's move forward.

Rev. Dr. Charles E. Goodman Jr.

Senior Pastor & Teacher

Tabernacle Baptist Church – Augusta, GA

INTRODUCTION

THE WEIGHT IS OVER

"Don't push me 'cause I'm close to the..." real music lovers, finish the rest! (Smiling big)

In a world that often feels both overwhelming and uncertain, we carry burdens—expectations, regrets, and fears—that can weigh us down so heavily that it feels like we are about to lose our heads. There is a transformative journey of self-discovery and liberation we embark on the moment we embrace the invitation.

Here you are. You're invited.

While navigating through my struggles, I learned that the heaviness of life can serve as both a weight and a teacher. Challenges became stepping stones, revealing truths about the power of resilience, authenticity, and choice. In this collective of those lessons (shared in the hopes that you, too, can shed the weights that no longer serve you), we will explore the foundational principles that guide us back to our core selves, confront the pain that shapes us, and embrace the inevitability of change.

Standing at the edge of a vast, open landscape where the horizon stretches infinitely before you, the sun rises, casting golden rays that illuminate the path ahead. This is an invitation to step forward. This is not a guide on how to change you. This is the moment I invite you to embrace as we begin sojourning.

Throughout my life, I often found myself carrying invisible burdens—weights of expectation, fear, and past regrets that anchored me to the ground. Like a traveler with an overloaded pack, I felt the strain of every choice and every unfulfilled promise. But in the depths of that struggle, I discovered a profound truth: the moment we unpack to lighten the load of all of the things we have unnecessarily carried—we reclaim our joy.

I wove a tapestry from the threads of my experiences, filled with vibrant colors of resilience, authenticity, and hope—unfolding like a new landscape, revealing insights gathered from moments of my pain, triumph, and everything in between. We will wander through the valleys of loss and the peaks of clarity, learning to shed the weights that no longer serve us.

Join me as we explore the beauty of returning to our roots, the inevitability of change, and the strength found in vulnerability. Together, we will uncover the power of loyalty, the freedom of authenticity, and the promise that even in our darkest hours, all is not lost. It's time to breathe deeply, feel the warmth of the sun on our faces, and step boldly into a life unencumbered.

The Weight is Over.

CHAPTER 1:

BACK TO BASICS

Back through the woods of my innocence, I recollect a conversation with my daddy about lifting my hands. I said, "Daddy, why do you always ask us to lift our hands at church?" He responded, "Well, baby girl, have you ever watched wrestling?" I sort of looked up, puzzled, and rhetorically went, "Ummmm... yeaaaaahh?" as it was a pastime we often enjoyed with my brother.

He says, "Well, when you're in a wrestling match, do you know the way to let your opponent know that you aren't defeated?" I shook my head to gesture "Not exactly," and he responded, "The only way to let the enemy know you've not lost the fight is to lift your hands."

My father went on that day (as He often did), saying, "Did you know wrestling is in the Bible? We're all in a wrestling match between what our natural or human responses or desires are, and the spiritual part of us that loves God and wants to please Him." Scriptures from my father I can't forget... Ephesians 6:12: "For we wrestle not against flesh and blood, but against principalities, against powers, against the rulers of the darkness of this world, against spiritual wickedness in high places."

My father continued: "If we are honest, sometimes the adversities of life make it hard to motion a sign of victory... but sometimes, the only way we can let our opponent, the devil, know that we are not defeated is by remembering to lift our hands to The Lord."

From that day forward, lifting my hands was no longer limited to just a sign of surrender, but of rescue, which I grew to understand as the safety of complete submission.

In my house, it was taught to me that respect was obedience, and anything contrary to that was primarily viewed as disrespect. My father was the voice of our home, and there was zero tolerance for this "disrespect" toward him and my mother. Growing up, my father was playful but also very strict, and if playing around went too far, there was never a moment he didn't issue out an opportunity for you to be disciplined. A standard of excellence was instilled that could not be negotiated.

My mother and father have always had extremely high expectations for their children. Failure was a thing made unacceptable in my house. The thought of it upset my parents. They professed sheer confidence in my abilities because of their own and refused to settle for anything less than my best.

I took a bunch of "whoopins," as the eldest of five (at that time), but I showed my tail more than once, and it gave me so much to write about—so it all worked out! And here we are.

Proverbs 22:6:

"Train up a child in the way he should go: and when he is old, he will not depart from it."

Here's the secret you've been waiting on: I lost sixty-eight pounds of excess weight through the wisdom of God and the faith that God is STILL the God of the Bible whom my parents introduced me to. I fell head over heels in love for the first time at twelve years old with Jesus, and all I have ever wanted to do since was make Him proud.

What are you waiting on God to do that you can fix through a little more discipline? What are you complaining about that you have the power to change? I realized yesterday (while resting in borrowed space) that the reason the Lord stripped me of everything was because I walked around as if nothing or no one could crush me. I was truly arrogant.

Early into my adult life, I took chances just to challenge myself. If I had known the blessings that awaited me would already be challenging enough, I would not have tired myself trying! But every challenge propelled me forward and ultimately became the strength for the journey.

Do you ever wonder what events in history, preceding the events of your own life, helped shape the unending narratives and overall perception of others? In a society primarily shaped by the fancied narratives of technological advancements and social media platforms, I think it is time we got back to basics.

I was today years old (as they say) when I fully understood why I heard so many churches folk in the hood and in the country start testimony service with (fill in the blanks)— "I give honor to ___ who is ___ ___ ___ ___ ___. I want to thank him for my ___, ___, and ___. I want to thank Him for being ___, ___, and ___ with the ___."

If I could sum up my journey with one word, it would be "grateful." There are not enough adjectives to describe how grateful I am to God for His unfailing love for me. I surely don't deserve it, even though I have been found guilty of indirectly taking His love for granted. Yet, I'm grateful for the gift of the Holy Ghost.

The beginning of any story is strategic. Even the beginning of your story was strategic and predestined by God. I'd like to break bread with this food for thought: How were you in the beginning?

I must have been about three and a half or four years old, just old enough to realize that the days of curling up in my mother's lap and falling asleep during church were behind me. Instead, I was given a piece of paper and a pen, which is how I first started drawing—quietly sketching as my tiny fingers explored the edges of the wooden pew.

I remember sitting there, tracing my fingers along the smooth, worn handles of the bench in front of me, my little hands gliding back and forth as the hum of the Leslie from the B3

Organ filled the air. My great-great Aunt Alice, always dressed in crisp white gloves, sat nearby, her hands trembling slightly from arthritis. I didn't fully understand why she moved them so gently, then something in the room changed.

It wasn't the usual rhythm of the church anymore. The air grew thicker, heavier, charged with something unspoken. I could feel it even then—an unmistakable shift in the atmosphere. The congregation was no longer just sitting passively; they were alive with worship. Voices rose, a chorus of prayers, shouts, and praises. People stood, swayed, rocked, or knelt—some with tears flowing freely.

But the one sound that pierced through it all was my grandfather's voice, the charismatically unique and commanding tone of Bishop Spight, calling on the name of Jesus. "Come on, saints! Call His name! Jeeeeeesus! POWER! In the name of Jesus... HEALING when you call Him... DELIVERANCE in that name... SALVATION when you call Him..." His words rang out with authority, filled with the kind of conviction that seemed to shake the very air.

Without thinking, I stood up from the front row. My voice joined the others, a small child's voice calling on the name of Jesus—over and over, the sound of it both innocent and desperate. I wasn't just repeating words; I was reaching for something, something I knew was beyond me, or my role as a preacher's kid—but something I was meant to touch.

The more I called His name, the more the world seemed to disappear. A wave of chill swept over my body, like cold fingers brushing my skin, but it was far from uncomfortable. It was as if I were being wrapped in a big warm blanket of safety and comfort.

Then it came—the presence. It wasn't just a feeling; it was an undeniable, all-encompassing knowing. A joy so deep it made my heart ache with its beauty, a love so profound it left no room for doubt. I can't explain it—because it wasn't something I understood with my mind—but it was as though my soul had finally met the One it had been longing for, even before I had the words for such a longing. And in that moment, I knew: He was real, and He was there.

Ecclesiastes 12:1: "Remember your Creator in the days of your youth, before the days of trouble come and the years approach when you will say, 'I find no pleasure in them.'"

I remember when I was in kindergarten and one of my best friends in my class dared me to "moon" the class. Can you believe it? She dared me to pull my pants down and show my tail! So, you know what I did, right?

The only African American teacher I ever had (until high school)—Mrs. Garmen—did not play. She was an old-school teacher that my mom permitted to get on to me before I even got home. Mrs. Garmen called home and told my mother what I'd done. Touch your neighbor and say, "...and that was the beginning." When my mom came to pick me up from school, she acted so sweet that I thought she had forgotten what I did. But she was silent when we got in the car (even after I'd created conversation—which, believe it or not, I rarely did) because she said the words that made me nearly lose my bladder: "When we get home, you're going to get it." Touch your neighbor and say, "And it happened!"

See, like Jesus, my parents were promise keepers. My parents raised and structured my life in the fear and admonition of the Lord. They understood that by helping me to value the principles of God, building a life on those principles would produce an indestructible foundation. Finding a love so unconditional, so unwavering, so sublime has changed my life forever. Introducing me to Jesus was the best gift they could have ever given me.

It's complex, but it's "basic" to most, simply because we have heard it before, so there is little honor or reverence for the selfless sacrificial seeds of prayer your forefathers watered in tears. The more I accept life as God's way of watering me, the more I grow able to see the picture of God's purpose for every moment in time, stretching back to His creation. The beginning sets a precedence for the operation of God's divine order.

As of 2023, The Lord of the Rings has been ranked the seventh highest-selling novel in the world. The Quran has sold over 3 billion copies, but still, the number 1 selling book for over 500 years—since 1522—the Christian Bible has remained the highest-selling book of all time (and the best part is, it's nonfiction). Selling over five billion copies, the "Holy Bible" is also the least-read book in America today.

As an aspiring anthropologist, I've come to discover that there are many places in the world where modern-day Christians are currently being persecuted for having a Bible in their possession—but (fun fact)—not in America! Ninety percent of people (this includes professing Christians) do not read the Bible. Many of the other church-going ten percent are not willing to admit how often they only pull out the Bible at Sunday morning services or Bible study. Yet the Bible remains one of the greatest works of literature ever produced.

While studying time's progression, I'm certain that even if you hesitate, you'll yet concur with me that culturally, many of us have subconsciously developed a tolerance for this generation's lack of biblical literacy. Without fully realizing it, even as both Bible readers and believers in Jesus Christ, we've often refrained from redepositing simple Bible knowledge to our children when, in fact, art, music, and literature were all inspired by the Bible.

Over time, the world has changed very much, but this sheer fact remains: even the many laws that govern this world are based on the Bible. The only book that has action, drama, is a thriller, romantic, historical, heart-racing, mysterious, and comedic—the Bible, the greatest story (that isn't a story but the truth) ever told. God's word is, was, and has always been both the ultimate foundation to build on and the most essential barometer for measuring success.

Jon Luke Godard said, "A story should have a beginning, middle, and end, but not necessarily in that order." The enemy has been trying to omit my existence before I was even born. My mother was young and not yet married when she conceived... some suggested it was not time for me to arrive.

I remember not being able to speak above a whisper at the Children's Hospital... I remember my little yellow nightgown with the balloons all over it and the cold IV that would flush my veins while being hooked up in the hospital for weeks because of pneumonia at age six.

In February of 2014, I experienced what many would call a "freak accident" when I slipped on ice, hit the back of my head, and had a concussion. I was on a flight when the landing gear broke while we were in the air a few years ago.

When the enemy's attempts to destroy me with other devices didn't work, I went through a season of depression; but Satan realized he wasn't powerful enough to kill me. That's when he tried to convince me that I would be better off just killing myself! (Shaking my head) But I couldn't die until destiny was fulfilled in my life!

Today, God, I thank You for the greatest gift: life, and that abundantly! Take a moment and reflect: Everybody has a testimony... what is your story? There's a beginning and a middle, but as long as you are alive, all is not lost because, like a semicolon, the story is not over yet.

Judging by the initial chaos, confusion, disarray, and disorder depicted in the beginning (Genesis 1:1-2), as the scripture unwraps, we can't help but notice how synonymously the days of creation have the same amount of time regardless of what God chose to create that particular day. Each day (containing both day and night) made the basics not so basic. Although people make getting to God so complicated, the complexities of God are so unique that...

Diving deeper, we come to understand that (John chapter 1) before God ever spoke a word, "In the beginning was the Word, and the Word was with God, and the Word was God, and the same was in the beginning with God. All things were made by Him, and without Him, there was nothing made. In Him was life, and the life was the light of men, and the light shineth in darkness, and the darkness comprehended it not."

The Bible reveals that God is not bound by the metrics of time, or at least how we view it as human beings. We understand, per exploring the Bible, that the angels were created before the earth, according to Job 38:4-7—therefore so was Lucifer, the worshipping angel who was kicked out of Heaven due to his defiance of God's rule over him. This made him the highest-ranking thief, robber, and murderer in history.

Since the beginning, Satan has come to kill, steal, and destroy you because of these three things:

- **Your Position**
- **Your Priorities**
- **Your Power**

Lucifer was the chief worship leader in Heaven. He was the most beautiful and most luminous angel. He had a high-ranking position in the angelic host. He was full of wisdom, described as an "anointed, powerful angelic creature, worthy of surrounding the throne of God" (Ezekiel 28:12-17).

But when Satan was condemned to hell, he was no longer able to worship. He was no longer beautiful or wise. He was no longer anointed. He no longer had a position, he no longer had priorities ordained by God except to destroy you. But most importantly, he no longer had power.

I must encourage somebody who's been asking life, "What do you want from me?" — that even though you're being tested right now while following the instructions God gave you, **YOU MUST STAY IN POSITION, MAINTAIN YOUR GOD-GIFTED PRIORITIES, and REMEMBER YOUR POWER.**

I needed to remind some of you who are asking yourselves why the devil has been fighting you so hard these past eight months and you feel like giving up because you feel like you can't take life anymore, and you're just over it; God told me to tell you to stay in position. I know it's tough right now, but hang in there. I know it's overwhelming, but hang in there. I know it looks like chaos, but if you can just trust God enough to TRY HIM ONE MORE TIME, if you would just stay in position and focus on the things GOD has given you to do, if you can just be FAITHFUL IN FOCUSING ON HIM— God says, if you can just keep your mind stayed on Me, I'll perfect your peace! (Isaiah 26:3)

And if you could just not be distracted by who's not doing what you think they're supposed to be doing and just grab a hold of the Genesis anointing pulling on the inside of you, begin again seeking FIRST God's kingdom, and not your rightness, but His righteousness, then God, who sees and knows all, will add everything else. (Matthew 6:33) — IF YOU can be a good steward over the things I've given you rule over, if you could just not take for granted this opportunity you prayed for and trust Me to work out the rest knowing that God moves off obedience... and understand that although you feel tired and weak today, the race is not given to the swift, nor the battle given to the strong, but to the one that endures (Ecclesiastes 9:11) — if you could just use your spiritual weapons, remembering that you are a warrior, and although to whom much is given, much is required, God says, I have the power to help you overcome every intimidating mountain.

You can speak to the mountain, and say, "Be thou removed, be thou cast into the sea" (Mark 11:23), who are you, great mountain, that you should not bow low? — Greater is He that is in me than he that is in the world (1 John 4:4) — I can do all things through Christ who strengthens me! (Philippians 4:13)

The universe began with a symmetrical order, aligned, proportioned, and orderly. On the first day, God created light; on the second day, the sky; on the third day, dry land, plants, and trees. On the fifth day, sea and flying creatures; on the sixth day, animals on land, and finally, man and woman. Humans were the last thing God made, yet we are the only creatures made in the image and likeness of God.

It is shrewd to conclude that the created order of maleness and femaleness is not limited to how we identify humanity, but how we identify the divine image of God.

In the beginning, (the same day God made the animals) God took from the dust of the earth and created and formed man, breathed His breath into him, and instructed him first to work and maintain the land. Then, God showed Adam His creations for him to name and identify. It was then, after notifying Adam through creation that man was the only thing made without a pair, that God spoke to Adam again, saying, "It is not good that man should be alone; I will make a suitable helper for him." (Genesis 2:18)

God wanted Adam to clearly notice that, unlike any of the other things He created, Adam had no mate. So, the Bible says that God put Adam to sleep, and it was then, when Adam was asleep, that the Lord removed Adam's rib—the rib, a section of the cage that houses the body's most vital organs—specifically, the organs that house your lungs and other vitals that help you to breathe. The ribs protect the heart. God made Eve (or Eva in Greek; in Hebrew, Eve translates to mean "the living one" or "source of life"). After removing Adam's source of life, Oops, I mean rib (smiling), God sealed Adam back up. When He woke, I believe Adam recognized the piece of himself, now wrapped in walking flesh. He crashed into his DNA (which was the makeup of God in another form like him—the part of Him that was missing, the piece of Him that belonged closest to his heart, to act as part of the house that protected the heart and lungs). What was missing had been found, and so Adam said, "WOAH MAN! She was taken out of me!"—"THIS is bone of my bone, flesh of my flesh!" (Genesis 2:23)

Fast forward to the garden, God spoke to Adam... and then Adam spoke to Eve... and then Eve spoke to the enemy. This is a clear depiction of how Satan uses sin, or going against the order of God, to separate us from God and keep us in bondage. It is by deceiving and tempting us to be out of order with God that the enemy knows he can keep us from receiving what God has for us.

It was not ironic that the snake never spoke to Adam, because the enemy is keen in his little devices. Satan comes by way of a snake and tempts Eve in the garden by telling her, "You will not surely die." Eve chose to believe the father of lies because her faith was too little to believe the word of her Father in heaven, which was sent by way of her covering!

I yield to superior authority in reverence to where I am submitted. I prophetically decree, according to Job 22:28, that says, "Thou shalt also decree a thing, and it shall be established unto thee, and the light shall shine upon thy ways"— that God is giving you the wisdom, will, and discipline to be free from a life of self-centeredness. I decree that as you begin to submit to God's authority, there is a new order being established in the realm of the spirit concerning you and your connections, and it's a spirit of "Yes" to the will of the Lord, a spirit of total obedience to God spiritually, physically, financially, and emotionally. A greater hunger for excellence and righteousness, freedom from complacency and timidity, and a launch into holy boldness and readiness.

I don't know about everybody, but this one is for the believer that's hungry for restoration, for the believer that's ready for the abundance, for the believer that says, "God, I'm ready for a second wind. If You give me just a little more patience, I'll do what You want me to—the hard thing—the uncomfortable thing. I refuse to settle for mediocre." But we must come into alignment with what God has called us to! The season may change, and the assignment may grow, but the priority must always be God.

If we really want to see the manifestation of God's glory revealed in our lives by way of the irreversible blessings God has commanded concerning us, sowing—by staying committed to a life of service and sacrifice—must be a priority. It's part of the basics.

When you submit yourself to the ways of God, you experience the will of God. I don't know about you, but I can't afford to miss God's intention concerning me. I've got some loved ones that I need God to save. I've got some areas of my life that need God's healing. I've got some struggles that I need God to bring me out of. We must seek to have a spirit of endurance that says, "I've been through too much!" "I've prayed too many prayers!" "God's been too good to me after all I've been through!"

I dare you to get bold and take every thought captive that tries to exalt itself above the knowledge of God. Talk back in the spirit realm and tell the devil, "For God I live, and for God I die." It will give Satan a black eye if your posture is praise, no matter where you are in this moment. Just for about two point five seconds, shout, "Thank you, Jesus!" Because God gave you time when He woke you up this morning to get in alignment. This time, we are staying in position.

Circumstances may have tried to distract you and take your position, but take back your rightful place. Use your authority by continuing to show up. Purposefully love your enemies. Keep sowing in the dark. It gets hard to see your way out sometimes, but keep pressing through the pain. Stay committed. Your destiny and your legacy depend on alignment with the order of God.

I, therefore, from this day forward, give my best, live my best, and am my best. These days, family, I acknowledge that the devil hates me. But it's all because I took his position as a worship leader. I am in charge of his former priorities (which are praising and him now) (laughs).

Jesus left the good Comforter—the Holy Spirit, the power of God at work in us. Power in the Greek means dunamis, which means to make possible that which was not so. The same power that raised Jesus from the dead is raising up a renewed power inside of you. You're not too old—God used Abraham. You're not too suicidal—God used Elijah. You're not too abused—God used Joseph. You're not too broke—God used Job. You're not too unintelligent—God used Moses. You may be afraid, but you can trust God and do it scared, and just like Gideon, God will use you too.

If your husband passed away, you're not just a widow—God was with Naomi! You are not too far from God. He chases after the one He loves. God proved that when He found Jonah. You're not too dirty—God used Rahab. You're not too evil—God used David. But moreover, the same power that raised Jesus from the dead... In case you needed to be reminded, if that wasn't enough, and you never make it through the first page of the Bible to check out the beginning, that same power God had to speak—and there was—this is the very power working in you.

It is time for the "Out Of Order" sign to be removed. So today, let's put this thing to use. Say this with me: "I will be more intentional than ever in pursuit of purpose. I will no longer procrastinate or complain. I will no longer mismanage and avoid. I receive what has belonged to me since the basics."

CHAPTER 2:

IRREVOCABLE TIME

Verse 1:

I can show ya better than I can tell ya

No clue what you're in for, they don't tell ya

Pre-Hook:

Have you ever been through the tests? I mean, all the way through the tests.

I took the scenic route through the tests.

Steady, tunneling through the tests.

Okay, enough going through the tests.

Look up, and I'm going through the test.

It's like I always go through the tests,

When I go through the tests of time.

— Alexis Spight

I try not to be over-cautious, but because I'm very big on the importance of time—(in that it is irrevocable)—sometimes my answer to even the most intriguing things today is "No," even before agreeing to find out what the endeavor is like.

Furthermore, I re-analyze certain decisions I make in life often and think: This is why I was initially opposed... Because various contributing factors push me to cognitively question the waste of my time. You know that old saying about time—it's true: once it is gone, you never get it back.

Now, don't get me wrong—I don't want to ever miss out on potential bliss by overthinking... Or operating in unintentional ignorance... However, I am not in a position where I can afford to make hasty decisions that later lead to a waste of time—time that I'll never be able to get back. Time is an investment, and without divine redemption, you can never get it back.

When I make this known to the people in my life, I expect them to respect that... As I would their time. You are probably laughing at me like "That's not realistic..." or perhaps your sentiments align?

I naturally do my best not to ever put a person in a compromising position regarding taking advantage of their time. There are many moments in time, however, that test us.

The tests of time always reveal unanswered questions. Questions that frame the confounds of our destiny linger in our waiting. Because of the countless errors I made while trying to balance the ignorance of the details that come with new seasons and unfamiliar territory, for a while, my temporary disposition forced me into thinking that I may have missed out on the opportunity to be who I believed God called me to be because I made the wrong choices.

I made bad investments. I did not always spend my time investing in learning, but rather entertaining parts of myself. For years, after countless losses (many at my own commission and others of omission... it did not matter), I beat myself up.

Though I am blessed to have accomplished many things with the help of the Lord, I like to limit my introduction to being a lady with red hair who loves God. The hair? I call that the fire reflecting on the outside what I cannot put out, inside.

My short, though eventful tenure of just a little over three decades here on earth has created a tremendous appreciation for even the least of things. Similar to Paul's sentiments in Philippians 4:12-13:

"I know how to get along with humble means, and I also know how to live in prosperity; in any and every circumstance I have learned the secret of being filled and going hungry, both of having abundance and suffering need. I can do all things through Christ who strengthens me."

Another attribute indicative of who I am is that I know no stranger—I love people. I always have.

The Weight is Over

It's the reason no one ever believes that I am, preferably, more introverted. I tend to be a naturally lovable, friendly, and nurturing being. Being a preacher's kid and the eldest of seven, I believe, was preparation for the journey God has me on now—serving and pouring into others daily, with the ability to engage with a variety of cultural and ethnic differences.

As a Black woman, I cannot express enough my admiration for what God did when He made men. While I acknowledge the complexities of gender dynamics and the importance of honoring all individuals in their unique struggles, allow me this courtesy—this ode—to men.

In a world where men are often emasculated and diminished by society, government, and media, I stand in awe of the strength, resilience, and quiet dignity that many continue to display. Despite the heavy pressures placed upon them, they remain providers, protectors, and pillars within their communities. Their hard work, sacrifices, and emotional depth often go unnoticed—but I see you. I celebrate you. Men, in all your complexity, deserve recognition for the contributions you make and the quiet courage you carry daily. I am truly grateful for the amazing men of God in my life who have my back. I could not be who I am without you.

Now, while I hold deep admiration for many men—there is one man I cannot seem to get along with. Never have. You may know him. His name is Old Man Trouble.

He also answers to "stress," "incidents," and "bad news."

Old Man Trouble's visit to me in 2003, in my hometown of Buffalo, New York—though considered a mild year, temperature-wise—was chilling in every sense.

I remember that November vividly. We accumulated nearly a foot of snow. The air was heavy with dampness, and to us, it felt like the coldest winter ever. That same season, our water heater froze, and our furnace gave out. After multiple attempts by my father to manually relight the pilot, it still wouldn't catch. With no heat and no hot water, confined to the indoors by the freezing outdoors, we defaulted into God's plan for us to stay inside.

The fireplace stayed lit. The oven stayed on. The electric heaters stayed plugged in. Toes and necks, tucked.

I remember one morning, my father bundled in layers of scarves and clothes, hovering over the electric stove—making hot grits, hard scrambled cheese eggs, crispy Applewood-smoked bacon, and hot biscuits for the five of us and my mother. I watched him—his calloused palms rubbing together, blue fingertips tucked into the seams of layered pants, pacing in double socks and sneakers. If there were ever a chef's edition of Survivor, my dad could've taken the win.

The condensation escaping his nose and mouth with each breath looked like smoke from a fire. Watching from a distance, eyes wide with wonder, I saw my fire-breathing old man and suddenly took off upstairs to round up my four younger siblings.

He caught a glimpse of me mid-run—and smiled.

That smile overwhelmed his face.

And my exhausted heart? It found rest that night—inside that smile. That smile confirmed what I needed to know: Old Man Trouble was no match for my Old Man.

I discovered early on that suffering is inevitable. You can't go under it. You can't go around it. You will get over it—but you must go through it.

Chris Stanley once said, "Adversity is always unexpected and unwelcome. It is an intruder and a thief. And yet, in the hands of God, adversity becomes the means through which His supernatural power is demonstrated." That stuck with me.

You see, our response to suffering influences how quickly we are established. There's an art to suffering. That's right—there is a way to suffer. Mastering that art, learning how to suffer well, is key to becoming fruitful.

1 Peter 5:10 says: "But the God of all grace, who hath called us into His eternal glory by Christ Jesus, after that ye have suffered a while, make you perfect, establish, strengthen, settle you."

This scripture suggests that God's perfecting work in us comes through suffering. And in any formula for success, every step matters. Omit one, and the result changes. So it is necessary—vital—to trust the process.

What gave me pause were those words: "a while."

If suffering only lasts "a while," yet seems to visit us routinely—when considering God's affection and purpose—it becomes clear: suffering is not punishment. It is preparation.

Oh, to be prepared.

In our youth, and even now as sons and daughters of God, we often grow impatient. But when we begin to understand the intention behind the trials—when we accept the art of suffering as divine refinement—then even Old Man Trouble becomes a character in the story of our becoming.

Does anybody remember staying up throughout the night just to watch the sunrise? (Smiling) That was back in the day when we played outside until the streetlights came on and drank from water hoses. Times have certainly changed. Today, we live in a society that has conditioned us into a microwave, "just add water," "set it and forget it," "can't wait," "can't sit still," fidget-spinner mentality when it comes to waiting on the blessings of God.

Like Abraham and Sarah, we often try to take our futures into our own hands, hoping to help God fulfill His promises a little faster—not realizing that God is already on the verge of pulling our blessings out of spiritual marinades, ovens, and crockpots. He's been slow-cooking something incredible on our behalf.

God promised Abraham that he would become the father of many nations. But when Sarah remained barren, both grew impatient. In attempts to protect themselves and force God's hand, they manipulated situations. On two separate occasions—once in Egypt and once in Gerar—Abraham and Sarah lied, claiming she was his sister rather than his wife, fearing for his life because of her beauty. Still, God protected Sarah both times and reaffirmed His promise.

Their most notable misstep was when Sarah, still childless, suggested Abraham have a child with her servant, Hagar. This led to the birth of Ishmael. Yet God, in His faithfulness, declared that Sarah would indeed bear a son—Isaac—through whom the promise would be fulfilled. Despite their attempts to expedite God's plan, His divine timing prevailed. This is a reminder that it's not enough to have faith—we must also have patience in trusting God's promises.

(Genesis 12:10–20; 20:1–18)

If we venture back a little further in Scripture, Isaiah 42 reveals the suffering of Israel due to their disobedience. But then, Isaiah 43 opens with hope: "But now…" After the devastation of the previous chapter, a new dawn breaks—just like the sunrise we used to wait all night for.

The beauty of Isaiah 43 is that it comes from a place of captivity. Isaiah was in bondage when God reminded His people of His covenant. Imagine that—being in a shutdown season. A complete rhythm shift. Maybe you're out of that season now, but don't forget where God brought you from. Or maybe you're in that season now. If so, don't you dare give up—God hasn't given up on you.

I thank God for being in covenant with us—not contract. Contracts, as I've learned in my journey as a serial entrepreneur and nonprofit founder, can be broken when one party is in breach. I'm grateful for amazing people in my life like my phenomenal attorney, Dr. Gregory Daniel—whom I affectionately call "Dr. Greg." He's helped me understand the ins and outs of contracts. But unlike contracts, a covenant is unbreakable. It's God's eternal commitment to us. No matter what, He says: "I am going to be with you."

(Deuteronomy 31:8; Hebrews 13:5)

That truth changes everything. It doesn't even matter where we go—He reaches for us. "If I ascend to heaven, thou art there: if I make my bed in hell, behold, thou art there."

(Psalm 139:8)

A wise man once said: "It's not what I go through that determines my success coming out, but what I do while going through." Let us be found trusting, waiting, and walking in faith while we go through.

Bearing in mind the fact that the Lord never leaves us, we must find the will to be tenacious—even through adversity.

We must not be disillusioned, persuading ourselves with the idea that, for any reason, we ought not to be blindsided by trials. Trials come with the territory of being a believer in Jesus Christ.

There is a misguidance being shared in many churches today. Due to the popularity and religiosity of what is known as the "Prosperity Gospel," and the negligence to focus on a full "Kingdom mindset," many think that the moment we make a decision to be souled out for God, bad things stop happening.

Don't beat me up, okay? I want peace! (Laughs)

I think you're hungry though—like me. Let's take a break for lunch really quick.

The word "when" in Isaiah 43:2 is an indication of God's omniscience—He already knew the timing in which we would pass through troubled waters.

We have to be confident in God's ability to be God for us, especially when His word lets us know that, although it's new to us, He already knows the outcome.

Anne Graham Lotz said, "When we are facing an impossible situation, all self-reliance and self-confidence must melt away; we must be totally dependent on God for the resources."

As disciples of Christ, it is the will of God that we aim to be disciplined believers. In aiming to be disciplined, we must work habitually in an attempt to stay focused amid Satan's tactics to destroy, disrupt, and distract us from seeing the promises of God already manifesting in our lives.

Oftentimes, we try to make sense of why we are experiencing trials—browsing for someone to hold responsible. Without recourse, many of us (like I once did) blame our past mistakes, wrong decisions, and bad choices for our suffering—without recognizing an insurmountably extreme moment as an opportunity for God to work miracles.

Vonette Bright said, "While chastening is always difficult, if we look to God for the lesson we should learn, we will see spiritual fruit."

While striving to emulate the example of Christ, it is fundamental that you grab a tight grip on the suffering Christ himself endured—even before the Crucifixion.

1 Peter 4:12 says, "Beloved, think it not strange concerning the fiery trial which is to try you, as though some strange thing happened unto you."

This means that if Christ suffered—even as the Son of God— we should find strength in thinking the way Christ did.

Reaching for 2 Timothy 2:12, we are encouraged by the idea that "if we suffer, we shall also reign with Him."

We must be confident in knowing that the challenges we face in life are no match for God.

Bishop J. Drew Sheard II said it best: "It is time we stop telling God about the mountain and tell the mountain about our God."

My family's furnace that winter of 2003 in Buffalo was never repaired. The brisk outdoors never warmed. The moist wind never dried. The water heater never unthawed. And Old Man Trouble's visit? It never shortened.

I learned early from that experience that true strength frequently involves remaining focused. According to the Word of the Lord in Hebrews 11:1, "Sight is perception of your present, but vision is faith for your future."

Often, we have no understanding of God's tactics—especially when they don't align with the promises He's given. Nevertheless, we must be careful not to allow pride to override wisdom.

Wisdom will come to you through the unlikeliest of sources—often through failure.

Aristotle said, "One is what he or she repeatedly does."

With the plethora of disappointments life's deck of cards constantly deals out, it is clever to suppose that winning should be a habit.

Change is inevitable. Essentially, we must learn to place sole confidence in God—the Author and Finisher of our faith, and our Chief Orchestrator. (Hebrews 12:2)

I've been gracefully pursuing the maintenance of my body and constantly working to achieve a lifestyle of health and fitness. On this journey, I've learned (through both exercise and study) that muscles are always developed through resistance. More often than not, our moments of immense opposition are the very moments God uses to cultivate us.

True stamina periodically involves asking for help and/or surrendering your will to fix it on your own.

It is therefore valuable to keep a servant's towel bigger than that of your ego.

The ego is the sedative that deadens the pain of ignorance.

As the snow piled heavily upon our door stoops and rooftop during Old Man Trouble's visit in 2003, so did our optimism—that perhaps, things could have been another way. I wondered for years why my Old Man smiled at me that morning while fixing breakfast for his family of seven in a house without heat or hot running water.

One might suggest it was the electricity that enabled the use of our electric heaters and stove to make warm meals, or maybe it was the blankets that bundled our necks and toes. Perhaps it was his gratitude for the walls that confined us, offering shelter from the storm.

Fishing for answers, I've since surmised that smile engulfed his round face for two reasons: his callused palms and blue fingertips. Those big hands... although very cold, had feeling—and that feeling meant life was in those hands, and thus, in him.

As long as we are alive, we've got time for God to complete the work He started!

Philippians 1:6 tells us, "He who began a good work in you will perform it until the day of Jesus Christ." When Old Man Trouble visits you, and you trust God enough to put your future in His hands, you relinquish your stead as pilot—allowing God to navigate the flight of your life faster, safer, and more efficiently than ever before.

God could have made us robots, controlled our every move, and eliminated our faults. But in His permissive will, He made us co-authors of our story—our choices shaping the outcomes that follow.

Success isn't measured by how much money we make, how hard we try, or even how well we handle life's curveballs. True success is found in the grace we experience through every decision we make, every lesson we learn, and every time we choose to trust Him.

When your steps are ordered by the Lord, you will be time tested—but time is never wasted.

CHAPTER 3:

INSURMOUNTABLE PAIN

Church thot

Thought you was a church girl, church hot.

Stop, girl. Work, girl.

You gon' get yourself hurt, girl.

And they gon' tell everybody and they mama for a surprise.

Yeah, you gon' be the number one topic in the headlines.

And your mama gon' cry so bad the pressure burns her eyes.

It's gon' be some truth—but it's all gon' be tied in lies.

Always been just a church girl, dreamin' from the B-lo.

That's why I'll always be low.

I hated when folks told me to stay humble,

Like I was ever the one tryna rumble.

I'm too free—like a girl cub in the jungle.

But still...

The Weight is Over

I hope you prosper in all your ways and sing on even bigger stages.

I hope you land a job one day, makin' even bigger wages.

I wish you well.

I wish you well.

I wish you well.

Your face came to mind one time, on my way home,

Like some kids in the heat after school,

Waiting to get in the kiddie pool.

I thought feeling free was a mutual feelin' that night,

'Cause normally—we could never be chillin'.

Sermons and songs, famous on stage.

Everybody knew and loved us our age.

Thought we were takin' over—hashtag elevate.

Finally in a crew where the slew of the stew

Had something to lose too.

Never thought anybody would snooze.

So... we had a few drinks and things got rotten.

But I'm still thinkin' all was forgotten.

The Weight is Over

'Til a couple weeks later, it was reported—

That they had that craziness recorded.

Now I'm a grown woman, and I own up to mine.

There's been a couple times I prayed for time to rewind.

I've made bad decisions, had my share of mistakes—

But I've owned all my flaws,

Like a big G—'cause Big G my boss.

So I never thought a Taco Tuesday

Would leave me with such a cost.

I take pride in that my name is all that I got.

So even if my career ends and my money shot…

Don't see me as a—

I'm so much more than—

One moment doesn't—

I'm more than my mistake.

My mother, after surviving the most embarrassing moment of my life and career, said to me:

"Curiosity still lingers in the air, an unspoken question on everyone's lips: What truly transpired?"

My past—like a shadow—reached forward, weaving itself into the threads of my future.

Insecurities can be insidious, whispering doubts that lead us down reckless paths,

Compelling us to act against our better judgment,

In a desperate bid for validation.

Confidence in my abilities was always a war internally.

I was confident… until I was rejected.

I've been different my whole life. I remember wearing funky high socks with suspenders and bowties (laughs). Intricately unique, indeed. But I wasn't always confident in it. I never quite identified with the victimhood often tied to the phrase low self-esteem, but I've certainly battled insecurity for a long time.

Being different was cool—until I realized it was unpopular.

I never tried to stand out. I just naturally did. Everywhere I went.

And I questioned God over and over, yearning to know His purpose in creating me so abstractly.

Before I ever appeared on television, I was working hard to make it as an independent artist—first capturing hearts on YouTube as a teen digital star shining bright from The Church of God in Christ. Then, the path led me to the bright lights of national TV.

Right before one competition, I had a conversation with a preacher who said,

"You know, there's a lot of people you aren't gon' reach because of that red hair and your crazy style of dress."

I looked at him—puzzled.

Slightly appalled.

So taken aback.

All my life, my uniqueness and authenticity had been affirmed—by my village, by the Word, and by the Christ-centered supporters who had shaped me. That comment stirred something deeper in me. I had an intense talk with God. I asked:

"God, what about the people who are just like me?

The ones who are eclectic and stand out?

The ones society tries to box in and can't quite figure out?

Who is going to reach them?"

Have you ever had a moment where you thought to yourself—

Yeah, man… I can sense the presence of God inside of me

Because we're always on the same wavelength?

The Weight is Over

I love it when I can see the power of God at work in me,

When my attributes reflect His nature.

One thing I love about myself is that I believe in using different methods to achieve different results.

I've learned—both through listening and through life—that doing the same thing repeatedly and expecting change is the definition of folly.

To continue on the same path without reflection…

Is to invite the same failures.

Change begins when we dare to break the cycle of our habits.

My doubts come in intervals—but they are often the result of my faith being tested.

And everywhere I look in scripture, I see that God raises up new individuals to fulfill His purposes—transcending conventional expectations.

In the moments I question my worth, especially because of projected societal labels, I go back to The Word and remember:

God loves to use the ones "they" named.

Let me remind you—

If God could use Esther, who many called "the orphan"—

Not realizing that her Persian name meant "Star"—

And that the Lord would raise her to become Queen of Persia…

Then surely, He can use me.

God often chooses the foolish things of the world to confound the wise.

So I prayed:

"God, if my journey can help catapult those who are just as unique as I am into a deeper assurance in Your love…

Use me."

And with that prayer—instantly—God confirmed my very being.

From the beginning, I asked Him to give me a ministry that would transcend all barriers:

Race. Age. Gender. Even the walls between genres and industries.

Now—with over six million listeners in more than 150 countries—my journey is living proof of 1 Corinthians 1:27-29.

"God chose the foolish things of the world to shame the wise… so that no one may boast before Him."

The Weight is Over

"Overcoming poverty is not a gesture of charity. It is an act of justice.

It is the protection of a fundamental human right: the right to dignity and a decent life."

Joy Dish soap bubble baths.

Barney sheets.

Tan linoleum floors.

Fragrant incense in the air.

So many light memories that made our grass-less front yard before the stoop in the "projects" easy to ignore.

When my best friend U-U would come knock and ask my mom,

"Can they come out and play?"

Suddenly, those cold Buffalo bricks of our little apartment rose seven stories high with joy.

Bologna sandwiches.

Spaghetti.

WIC cereal.

Consistent.

And to this day—I cannot imagine any young parents with five children doing better than mine did in our situation.

They gave us everything they had—and they worked diligently to condition our minds to rise above the attributes that governed our environment.

Studies show that while parents provide essential care and guidance, additional figures in a child's life—grandparents, mentors, relatives, family friends—can offer unique advantages and perspectives.

I am earnestly grateful for my village—

Their unwavering support and love have been instrumental in shaping my journey and enriching my life.

"For as long as I can remember, I've had a knack for getting myself into trouble. Not intentionally—I often genuinely believed I was doing the right thing. But time and time again, I found myself 'out of order,' mostly because I was simply misplaced. It wasn't until later in life that I began to introspect and realized how much of that misalignment stemmed from where—and how—I was positioned in life.

As a little girl, maybe four or five, I loved playing 'house' with my younger siblings. My sister, only a year younger than me—my sassy, bossy Irish-twin—always insisted on being the 'mother' to my brother and me. (Even though I was older and had baby dolls of my own!) We didn't question it. She made the rules, and somehow, I became her child. And honestly? I still am in her mind, even though I'm technically her babies' auntie in REAL LIFE. (Laughs) And then there was my brother—Lord have mercy. He could never pretend the baby dolls were real. He'd throw them around or use them as action figures in wrestling matches. (Face palm) Who else had a football-obsessed, wrestling-loving little brother like that?

Reflecting on those innocent, carefree days at home brings such deep nostalgia. Do you remember when life was simpler—when your days were filled with joy, and your only concern was whether your imaginary family followed the rules? How long ago was that for you?

For me, things shifted in kindergarten. I remember a classmate asking to stay with me until I fell asleep. At the time, I didn't fully grasp what was happening. My mother wasn't the most affectionate person, but I had been exposed to physical affection at my babysitter's house, so the request didn't feel strange—until much later.

Parents don't always realize how certain gaps in their presence or decisions can lead to vulnerability. Whether through unvetted caregivers, lack of open communication, emotional neglect, or inconsistent behavior, the security children need to thrive can be unintentionally compromised. And so, for years into my adulthood, I carried the weight of a secret I never asked for. A burden that silently sprinkled itself throughout my life, unnoticed—until it wasn't.

Carrying a traumatic secret affects you in ways you don't immediately understand. You bury it to survive, but it resurfaces in the form of anxiety, irrational fear, emotional detachment, or even the inability to connect deeply. It was only when I started recognizing those patterns that I began healing. Recognition was the first step toward reclaiming my peace. There's freedom in naming what happened to you and seeking the spiritual and mental support necessary to move forward.

Turning childhood abuse into a testimony of faith isn't an easy journey—it's layered, sacred, and sometimes overwhelmingly painful. But as a disciplined believer and follower of Christ, I've come to understand that even the darkest experiences can be transformed through healing and grace. Healing begins where the silence ends. And though finding a new beginning may seem daunting, every step toward wholeness is a victory."

Ten Steps to Facilitate the Healing God Has Already Promised You—Starting Today

1. **Accept God's Love and Grace**
   Begin by fully embracing the unfailing love and grace of God. When you understand His grace, you begin to see yourself as worthy—worthy of healing, worthy of joy, and worthy of a beautiful life.

2. **By Faith, Be Healed**

   Jesus said in Luke 17:19 (KJV), "Arise, go thy way: thy faith hath made thee whole."

   Healing begins with faith. Pray, study scripture, and meditate on God's Word.

   Psalm 1:2 (NIV): "But whose delight is in the law of the Lord, and who meditates on his law day and night." Lean into verses like Psalm 147:3: "He heals the brokenhearted and binds up their wounds." There is deep comfort in knowing that your pain is not unseen by God.

3. **Find Support**

   Healing is not meant to happen in isolation. Surround yourself with a Christ-centered community—whether through a church, a godly pastor, a Christian therapist, or a prayer circle. The right community will remind you that you are not alone and that your story matters.

4. **Reframe Your Narrative**

   Instead of seeing your past as a chapter of pain, begin to see it as the soil from which your resilience, compassion, and strength have grown. Your scars may become someone else's survival guide.

5. **Use Your Experience to Change the World**

There is power in your testimony. Use it to uplift, educate, and inspire others. Advocate for those who don't have a voice. Let your pain become a platform. I'm living proof—it can be done.

6. **Forgive**

    Forgiveness is not about excusing the wrongs done to you—it's about releasing their power over you. Forgive them. Forgive yourself. This is how you walk in freedom.

7. **Develop Healthy Coping Mechanisms**

    Journaling. Creating. Counseling. Nature. Worship. Whatever helps you feel, process, and release—do it. These aren't distractions; they're lifelines.

8. **Grow**

    Your growth is part of your healing. Try new things. Learn. Explore. Develop your gifts. As you grow, you reclaim the parts of you that trauma tried to bury.

9. **Trust in God's Plan**

    Even when it doesn't make sense—especially when it doesn't—lean on the truth that God is orchestrating something greater. He is the Author and Finisher of your faith, and His plan includes restoration.

10. Serve Others

Serving others heals in ways that words never could. It brings joy, fulfillment, and purpose. When you pour from your overflow, it becomes a blessing—not a burden.

Let's be honest: the pain you've experienced is real. It's heavy. Many haven't survived what you've suffered in silence.

I was in the gym the other day when something hit me—while re-racking my dumbbells, the clank rang out loudly and turned every head. Isn't it funny how the heavyweights are always silent? And yet when they hit the rack, the whole room feels it.

That's how trauma works. We carry it quietly. We function with it. We bury it deep. But every so often, it echoes—loud and jarring—reminding us that it never left.

The silent battles of our past, no matter how deeply buried, still speak. But here's the truth: even if your childhood left scars, even if your voice was silenced or your trust was broken—God still has a plan.

There is a path toward healing, purpose, and redemption through faith, community, and growth. And I want to walk alongside you.

My existence is proof that embracing God's love and purpose can lead to healing so powerful, your suffering becomes the key to someone else's salvation.

I don't know what you've been silent about for all these years. I don't know the weight you've been carrying.

But God told me to tell you:

That sacrifice... that suffering... that unspoken pain—He's about to use it.

As a plane that lifts you.

As a vehicle that enables someone else's breakthrough.

As proof that nothing—absolutely nothing—is wasted in His hands.

If I'm being real with myself, I'll admit—as much as I want to be all the time... I'm not.

I'm not always strong. Not always composed. Not always full of faith.

But here's what keeps me grounded:

My brother tattooed something on his arm that changed me.

Matthew 19:26 — "But Jesus beheld them, and said unto them, with men this is impossible; but with God all things are possible."

That truth stuck to me like glue.

It reminded me that in moments of weakness, vulnerability isn't defeat—it's access. Access to God's strength. To His power. To the backup that comes when you're walking alone but never truly alone.

Even Jesus said in Matthew 26:53 (NIV):

"Do you think I cannot call on my Father, and he will at once put at my disposal more than twelve legions of angels?"

That verse gets me every time. I mean—twelve legions. That's divine backup, y'all.

The truth is, life is… inevitable.

I don't know about you, but I get challenged most when I'm forced to face what I can't run from. (Laughs)

Don't judge me—but some days, it gives off "that one person you pretend not to see walking toward you" energy. (Facepalm. Smiling.)

But real talk—accepting that we can't avoid life's hills, valleys, twists, and turns… that's where the peace starts.

So, hey... you.

Yeah, you—the one reading this and silently nodding. The one sorting through pain, wrestling with whether any of it was your fault.

Here's the truth:

Healing is possible.

Freedom is real.

And it doesn't come from closure, validation, or explanations—it comes from God.

The moment you realize that what happened to you doesn't define what's ahead of you, a shift takes place.

Not even your story defines you.

It's the journey of healing, the resilience you're building, and the grace you're walking in that will tell the real testimony.

So, give yourself permission today—to breathe, to believe, and to begin again.

Your future isn't found in your past. It's born in your becoming.

CHAPTER 4:
INEVITABLE LIFE

A wise man once said:
"It's not what a man goes through that determines his success coming out—it's what he does while going through."

That line changed everything for me.
Because the truth is, life *will* test us. But God, in His infinite wisdom, uses those tests to shape the character of who we are becoming.

While striving to remain strong in life's toughest moments, I've learned that God doesn't just develop our endurance—He develops our identity.

In a world obsessed with image, we've become experts at hiding behind tattooed smiles and silent tears. But let's be real—there are things in life we can't avoid.
We can't outrun the hurt. We can't edit out the brokenness.
And no matter how different our stories may be, we all share this truth: *we are human.* And being human means we're vulnerable.
Who would've thought being human would be the hardest part of being alive? (Laughing)
But God knew. And He gave us grace for it.

We won't always understand His ways—and that's okay. Success isn't about understanding. It's about obedience. It's about *staying the course*, especially when it would be easier to check out or turn away. (More on that in Chapter 8.)

If we're honest, every single one of us has felt lonely.
Afraid.
Overwhelmed.
Lost.
But the fact that you're still here? That breath in your lungs? That's proof that God isn't done with you yet.
Your presence means purpose. And all is not lost.

Don't let pride block your path to wisdom.
Wisdom doesn't always come from the obvious places. Sometimes it comes wrapped in unlikely people, hard conversations, or painful moments.
But it is *the* principle thing.

And here's what I've learned in my (still developing) journey: Opposition is often God's cultivation ground.
Suffering isn't something we can avoid. You can't go under it. You can't go around it.
But you *can* go through it.
And more importantly—you *must*.

Suffering isn't punishment. It's preparation.
It's how God perfects us.
In today's instant-gratification culture, we want microwave

blessings.
But God? He's an oven kind of God.
While we're trying to rush our futures, He's slow-roasting our blessings to perfection.

So what do we do?
We trust.
We lean into His timing.
And we resist the temptation to take matters into our own hands.

That's my goal now—not just success, not just survival.
But **spiritual discipline.**
Not just being a good person—but being a *submitted* believer.

When I was a child, I acted like one. But now, as a woman, my greatest ambition is to be disciplined in faith.
Jesus is my template—*the* template. The ultimate model of obedience and resistance, even when everything in Him could've chosen otherwise.

As imperfect people trying to make a difference, we have to guard ourselves. The enemy is strategic—he aims to destroy, distract, and derail us from our destiny.
Sometimes we want to make sense of our trials. We look for someone to blame.
We question if it's our own mistakes, our past, our failures that brought the pain.

But what if...
What if your lowest point is the perfect place for God to perform His greatest miracle?

You know what it's like to smile through heartbreak.
To fake it while you break inside.
To cheer for others while losing your own battles.

And still, you show up.
Still, you believe.
Still, you hold on.

That's strength.
That's resilience.
And that's the fruit of faith.

1 Peter 4:12 says:
"Beloved, think it not strange concerning the fiery trial which is to try you, as though some strange thing happened to you."
Translation?
You're not cursed—you're being *crafted*.

You are stronger than you think.
And not because life made it easy, but because you believed God enough to hang in there when it wasn't.

Resistance builds muscle.
And in the weight of it all, a strength you never knew existed was uncovered.

"Being labeled or judged as a young person—by media, parents and family, teachers, mental health professionals, and even 'church-minded' people—is something I'll never fully understand, even now as a grown adult. Perhaps that's why I serve as a Youth Pastor today.

It's impossible for me not to consider that a young person's actions may stem from deep trauma or abuse. Labels leave lasting impacts, which is why I believe the Lord calls us 'blessed' nearly 300 times in Scripture—to remind us of our identity in Him.

As I entered my teenage years and even into young adulthood, the labels projected onto me often rang louder than the voice of God I'd been taught to listen for at home. Rumors, side comments, whispers—every quirky, unique vibration of who I was became a source of speculation.

Unbeknownst to them, their assumptions went deeper than surface-level misunderstanding. I tiptoed through life, trying to avoid disaster and spectacle at every turn. But eventually, I realized that I would be judged either way. I discovered value—even virtue—in moments of inadequacy.

Looking inward, I whisper to my inner child, "They see promiscuity… but no one can tell you were exposed too early." This is the part of my story that rarely gets spoken aloud. And yet, it echoes in the lives of many.

No matter our circumstances or intentions, one theme I've found to be universally true is: life be life'n.

Understanding this reality helps us navigate our experiences with more grace and resilience. Change is inevitable. Life is marked by constant transition, and when we embrace that, we open ourselves up to growth. Ecclesiastes 3:1-8 reminds us, "To everything there is a season, and a time for every matter under heaven." This scripture reveals the cyclical nature of life—joy and sorrow, gain and loss—all serving a purpose.

Maturity means learning to see challenges not as punishment, but as invitations to grow. I hear my Bishop's voice even now, quoting James 1:2-4: "Consider it pure joy, my brothers and sisters, whenever you face trials of many kinds, because you know that the testing of your faith produces perseverance."

When we adopt this perspective, we begin to understand that trials don't just happen to us—they build us. And even in the chaos, God is in control.

The inevitability of life also reminds us of the hope of eternity. Though earthly things fade, Scripture reminds us of something more. In 2 Corinthians 4:17-18, Paul writes, "For our light and momentary troubles are achieving for us an eternal glory that far outweighs them all. So we fix our eyes not on what is seen, but on what is unseen."

The Weight is Over

That's the perspective shift: to focus not on what is breaking around us, but on what is being built within us.

I honestly don't know what I've experienced more—moments I thought my life was over, or moments I thought my suffering season was finally done… only to hit another rock bottom. Each time felt like a final chapter.

But I've learned that endings often mark the beginning of something new.

These painful experiences have forged my resilience. They've taught me that hope can emerge from the deepest pit.

Life is inevitably full of change, challenge, and the collision of joy and sorrow. But through a biblical lens, we discover strength, purpose, and an unwavering hope.

When we understand that trials can produce growth—and that God is with us through it all—we're able to journey forward with faith and resilience."

After two Billboard chart-topping albums with Music World Gospel in 2012, I moved to Houston, Texas at just 20 years old—with a whole lot of faith and very little of anything else. The end of my partnership with my former manager due to irreconcilable business differences left me stripped and searching. Yet, Houston offered the perfect place to start again—despite the grief, the loss, and the uncertainty.

Soon after relocating, I became a co-host on 90.9 FM KTSU's "The Go Radio Show," and not long after, I was awarded a scholarship to Kingdom Theological Seminary. But even as doors opened, I found myself desperately trying to replace everything that had been stolen from me—including the dream I felt slipping from my grasp.

Unable to fill the void, I became an emotional hoarder—traveling the world, crying out songs of worship from a broken place. I was preaching, singing, and leading while bleeding (Chapter 9). Spiritually, I was contaminating places where healing was supposed to flow from me. Still, God—like the good Father He is—graciously patched my leaking heart just long enough for me to complete each assignment. But over time, the constant pouring out with little replenishment led to severe spiritual drainage.

I couldn't hide the contamination anymore. Like the woman with the issue of blood, I found myself sneaking through the crowd—reaching out for help in the backs of churches, hoping someone would be sensitive enough to notice my silent cry. Hoping for a prayer... or maybe even a miracle.

As the eldest child of a pastor, with the love of God rooted in me since birth, my one true desire has always been to serve God and His people. But the emotional, mental, spiritual, and financial toll of ministry leadership is often isolating. Despite traveling the world, I longed for covering. I wasn't used to not having a pastor—I knew the power of spiritual accountability, guidance, and nurture.

After praying, God led me to minister at a church in Houston. I committed myself fully—serving, tithing, sowing. But after a year, the pastor told me that due to the complexities of my life, he didn't know how to pastor me. That moment stung. I needed shepherding more than ever.

With limited mobility after losing my car to Hurricane Harvey and grappling with forced self-management due to unforeseen business breakdowns, I was in a spiritual and emotional drought. Even as a strong believer, I had stumbled and survived a long, winding tour through "Right and Wrong Avenue"—with pit stops in both the Broome County Jail and the choir stand before I was even sixteen. God is a deliverer—never get it twisted. I still fight, but now I fight on my knees.

There's an anointing that comes from survival. Because I've been through it, I do things differently. And I believe the same for you.

Let me speak this over your life: Everything you've experienced has cultivated an anointing to do it differently this time around.

You may be in that place right now—the one that feels like rock bottom. But as someone once said, "Rock bottom is a great place to build a foundation."

Faith without works is dead. Hebrews 11:1 says, "Faith is the substance of things hoped for and the evidence of things unseen." Even in adversity, we must go after the things of God. "Without faith, it is impossible to please God." It isn't easy—but I want to please God now more than ever.

Faith is fully activated in my life. I'm not married yet, I don't have children yet—but I am completely submitted to God's purpose concerning me. It's anything He says. Anything He wants.

I've learned: you never really know how much faith you have… until it's all you have.

And I will never let go. I will die trusting in God.

CHAPTER 5:

A PROMISE IS A PROMISE

Growing up between Buffalo, New York, and various parts of the Southern Tier region of the state, I always had a lot of nicknames. My daddy named me Alexis—but at home, when things were chill, it was "Lexi" or "Lex."

Now, pardon my Ebonics, but I have to say this one for the people they tried to keep in the back: you know your people mean business when they call you by your government name and yell, "Come downstairs!" (laughs).

I had a young momma and daddy who were old school, though. I can still hear my mother saying, "Girl, who do you think you talkin' to? Don't you know I will smack the black offa you?" (laughs) Or, "You better shut ya mouth before I slap you into next week." Lawd, have mercy! See, those weren't threats—those were promises!

My daddy? A promise keeper. (Shakes head with a smirk.) My momma was too, but Daddy was more poetic—more subtle with his. He'd say things that shook my soul. (laughs) Like:

"You better quit playin' with me… or Ima make a believer out of YOU!" (laughs harder)

The Weight is Over

So yeah, I preferred just "Lexi" or "Lex." If you knew me, you knew those names. And yet, sometimes folks would try it. You know those people who call you by a nickname and you're like, "Hol' up nie... you don't know me like that. WAIT!" (laughs)

I remember being on the phone with a phone company once. The rep said, "Thank you so much for your patience, Miss Spight. May I call you Alex?"

Face palm.

"No ma'am. Ms. Spight is fine, thaaaannnks." (laughs)

But honestly, I had a bit of a "plight" with my first name. It summoned who I was. Later, I learned why I felt that way. I had the nerve to look up what "Alexis" meant—and found out it means "Defender of Mankind." So naturally, I started noticing how every time someone called my name, I'd throw on a mental superhero cape. I was ready to defend, fix, cover, or save somebody. Every. Time.

I remember teaching preschool. There was this special grace that came over me every time a four-year-old would call my name—for absolutely no reason except to get my attention. At first, I loved it. I was honored they called my name expecting a response. But eventually, I realized... they were undervaluing the mention of my name. Calling me just to call me. Wasting the power behind the name.

The Weight is Over

Now I hear you—"Amen Lex! The saints need to put some respeck on my name!"

But here's the real question:

How many times have we become common with Jesus?

How often have we subconsciously reduced Him to just a "higher power"?

Or the "big man in the sky we pray to when we get in trouble"?

How often have we taken His love and saving grace for granted?

Daddy used to say,

"Always got yo hand out tryna get something, but don't wanna give nun."

Then he'd follow it up with:

"When's the last time you just told me… thank you?"

Whew.

I don't know who this is for, but somebody reading this ought to just tell God thank you!

I'm talking to the grateful believer who can say:

It wasn't my bank account.

It wasn't my grades.

The Weight is Over

It wasn't my credit.

It wasn't my momma or my daddy.

I'm not rich…

I'm just blessed like this.

I'm not even that popular…

Jesus just knows my name.

And I'm so glad He made a believer out of me.

There were parts of my life that I felt I couldn't change.

I was lost, but He found me.

When I was broken, He fixed me.

When I was down, He picked me up.

When my back was against the wall, He still heard me.

When I called Him, He answered me.

When I needed help, He rescued me.

What I was born lacking, He created for me.

Every specific and essential thing I needed to succeed—was Jesus!

He approved me when I should've been denied.

The Weight is Over

I went to the doctor and got a negative report—but it was Jesus who healed me.

It wasn't "bae," but Jesus who held me and wrapped me in His loving arms.

He didn't just wipe my tears—He bottled them.

And used them to water my seeds that are getting ready to cause me to reap an abundant harvest with joy!

I don't know how...

I don't know why...

I didn't deserve it...

But just when I needed Him—Jesus showed up for me at the right time.

Consider the careful hand of a garden tended.

Each seed planted represents a promise, nurtured by faith and patience.

As seasons change, blossoms unfold in their time—vibrant and alive—

Reminding us that God's timing is perfect.

Even in the winters of our lives, when hope feels buried under snow and ice,

The Weight is Over

Beneath the surface, roots are growing... preparing for the inevitable spring.

A promise is a profound declaration—

A commitment that transcends mere words.

It carries weight, like a stone dropped into a still pond, creating ripples that extend outward.

When someone makes a promise, they are offering a piece of themselves—

A pledge to uphold their word.

A vow to stand by their intentions.

At its core, a promise embodies trust—

An invisible bond between the giver and the receiver.

Promises are rooted in expectation and hope.

The true essence of a promise lies in its fulfillment.

A promise unkept can lead to disappointment,

While a promise honored builds unshakeable equity.

It's a dance of integrity and accountability,

Where the act of keeping that word solidifies character and deepens trust.

Ultimately, a promise is more than just a word—

The Weight is Over

It's a commitment to be a person of integrity,

A reflection of one's values,

A testament to a bond.

In a world where certainty often feels elusive,

A promise remains a timeless, powerful anchor—

Reminding us of the strength found in both honor and loyalty.

Like me, I'm sure you too have experienced many broken promises in your life.

Every broken promise I have ever received taught me valuable lessons.

They've deepened my understanding of both trust and vulnerability,

Reminding me to value those who genuinely keep their word.

The idea that people are made to let you down

Can stem from a few deep-seated truths about human nature and relationships.

At our core, we are imperfect beings,

Shaped by our experiences, our fears, and our limitations.

Each person carries burdens, making it inevitable that we sometimes fall short of expectations.

While painful, these experiences have ultimately strengthened my resilience

And helped me appreciate the power of both honesty and commitment in my relationships.

We often place our hopes in others,

Believing they will fulfill promises or meet our needs.

Yet every person's journey is complex, and they may struggle with their own battles.

This can lead to misunderstandings and disappointments.

Societal pressures and expectations were significant influences on my career

As a gospel recording artist—initially creating a facade that I felt I needed to maintain.

When I failed to live up to this image—

Whether due to personal struggles or unforeseen circumstances—

I felt betrayed, and I was let down.

But I had to realize that my worth is not tied to the actions of others.

Wisdom has taught me the importance of fostering connections with those who share my values,

The Weight is Over

And establishing boundaries that protect my heart.

What I love about God is that He is the ultimate Promise Keeper.

In a world filled with uncertainty and broken commitments,

His unwavering faithfulness stands as a beacon of light—

Warming our hearts in a world that often feels cold and dark.

Each promise He makes is like a pavilion in the middle of life's raging storms—

Offering stability, shelter, and safety when everything around us feels chaotic.

God's promises are rich with depth and meaning.

They span from the assurance of His presence in our darkest moments

To the unshakable guarantee of grace and redemption.

This reliability brings a profound sense of peace—

Knowing that no matter the challenges we face, we can trust in His Word.

When He says, "I will never leave you nor forsake you,"

It's not just a phrase.

It's a lifeline—a promise we can cling to,

The Weight is Over

Providing comfort in moments of fear, doubt, or need.

God's promises invite us into a relationship

Built not only on trust but on expectation.

They encourage us to look up with hope,

Reminding us that He has a plan for our lives—

Even when the path ahead is unclear to us.

Isn't it amazing to know that we are never without guidance?

If there is anything I am more grateful for today than ever before,

It is the Lord's direction.

I've reached a pivotal place in my life—

A place where I cannot afford to misstep.

Because if I misstep...

I might miss out.

In my humanity, I don't always know which decision to make.

But even in that uncertainty, I'm grateful I serve a God who is faithful—

A God who guides me through the fog,

Lighting my way even when I can't see what's next.

The Weight is Over

What's truly remarkable is that God's promises transcend time.

They aren't bound by our circumstances,

Nor are they limited by the fleeting nature of human commitments.

From ancient hieroglyphics to modern personal triumphs,

His faithfulness has been written, witnessed, and experienced—

Over and over again.

His Word is forever.

Ultimately, each promise kept is a testament to His character—

Inspiring a greater confidence in me,

Knowing that I am never on my own.

CHAPTER 6:

ONLY A FAILURE CAN'T BE TAUGHT

Proverbs 12:1 – "Whoever loves discipline loves knowledge, but whoever hates correction is stupid."

I used to love playing with fire.

Literally.

I was obsessed with being able to control the power of a flame.

As a kid, I often entertained my siblings by moving my hands and fingers quickly through match flames and grill torches.

Watching their eyes fill with wonder and amazement, I felt so cool.

There you are—judging me again! (Laughs)

Or maybe I'm the one judging myself.

I've made so many stupid decisions.

Even though, since childhood, I've attended some of the best schools in the nation,

I have no doubt my actions have often been labeled... well, stupid.

The Weight is Over

But you see, life isn't about keeping a record of how many mistakes we make.

It's about learning from the mistakes we make.

Still, if you play with fire long enough, eventually something—or someone—gets burned.

My parents were working late one evening.

I was still just a kid.

Bored out of my mind and desperate to entertain my siblings,

I had a moment of twisted brilliance:

"Let's light a newspaper on fire."

We had exhausted every game we could think of.

I knew if I didn't come up with something soon, the night would dissolve into whining and complaints.

And come on—would it really be me if it wasn't a dangerous adventure?

I thought I was a fireologist (laughs).

I truly believed I had perfected the art of playing with fire.

So I struck the match and lit the newspaper.

Captivated by the dance of flickering flames through ink,

We gazed in awe as each letter on the page came to life.

The Weight is Over

There was something deeply exhilarating about the crackle,

The warmth of the yellows that reflected in our little brown eyes.

In that moment, I was the hero.

I was Superwoman.

The one in control of what others feared.

There's power in feeling in control.

Especially over something as wild and beautiful as fire.

Until… you're not.

Before I knew it, a gust of wind swept through our castle-like 1920s house in Niagara Falls, New York.

The front door had cracked open—

And the fire leaped.

My heart dropped into my stomach.

Panic gripped my chest as I realized:

I was not in control.

Not anymore.

My parents were home.

The damage was undeniable.

The Weight is Over

I scrambled, rushed to put out the flames,

Desperately trying to erase the mistake.

We filed into a horizontal line like little soldiers,

Frozen in place, awaiting judgment.

We were caught.

There was no escaping the consequences now.

The newspaper was gone.

The matches, hidden.

But there were remnants.

Ashes.

Smoke.

That distinct, undeniable odor of burnt regret.

Evidence lingered in the silence of the room.

By God's grace, there was little to no damage.

But the anger in my parents' eyes upon entering the room was... different.

It wasn't just anger.

It was disappointment.

And somehow, that hurt more.

The Weight is Over

There's a certain weight to hearing, "We're not angry... we're disappointed in you."

It was more than just a scolding.

It was about the recklessness.

The blatant disregard for safety.

The failure to respect a lesson they had spent years trying to teach me:

That fire—though beautiful—is dangerous.

And I had treated it like a toy.

Like I could control something more powerful than me.

In doing so, I nearly brought destruction to everything and everyone around me... including myself.

I had been too reckless.

Too arrogant.

Believing that because I could manipulate the flame, I was somehow immune to its consequences.

I underestimated its potential for harm.

I didn't think anything bad could actually happen.

But that day, I learned:

Fire isn't something you control.

It's something you respect.

"Without rules, there can be no consequences. Without consequences, there can be no reinforcement." – K. Francis Smith

That moment with the fire was my first practical lesson in understanding consequences. But it wouldn't be my last.

I was stubborn. Years later, I found myself in similar situations—not with literal fire this time, but with metaphorical flames: relationships, choices, opportunities, even my career. Every time I thought I could control the fire—whether by acting impulsively (sending that text message) or ignoring wise counsel (like getting my own attorney)—the heat would rise, and God would once again have to put out the flames.

To many people, I looked like either a renovation project or a demolition site. Looking back, I see a young woman eager to learn—but too proud to fully accept guidance. I wanted the good parts of God. I wanted the blessings, the favor, the freedom. I thought, "I'm grown. I've been taking care of myself since I was sixteen. I pay my own bills—nobody can tell me what to do."

But I didn't want the responsibility that came with it.

I wanted to believe it was God if it felt good. I built my reality on emotions, not truth—and that reality was often far from how God actually works. I was too quick to burn things down just to feel the thrill of the flames. But over time, after mistake upon mistake, I began to realize the real lesson wasn't in avoiding failure—it was in embracing correction when it came.

God was teaching me.

What if He's teaching you, too? What if that's exactly what this is?

Only someone unwilling to be taught is a failure. But those who are willing to listen, learn, and grow will eventually gain the wisdom to handle even the wildest fires—with grace.

"The fear of the LORD is the beginning of wisdom, and knowledge of the Holy One is understanding." – Proverbs 9:10

There's no real growth in trying to avoid failure. The growth is in being willing to learn from it. To sit in the consequences of your actions and ask, "Okay… what can I take from this?" Because the truth is—failure doesn't define you. It's your response to it that shapes you.

"Though the righteous fall seven times, they rise again, but the wicked stumble when calamity strikes." – Proverbs 24:16

"When are you going to learn?" That's what my mom used to say. And I swear, I felt life yelling a few of her quotes at me over the years. (Smiling) One time, life said, "You gon' learn today!" And I said, "Who you talkin' to? You are not my mom!" (Laughs)

But you know what? You can smile now—the hard part is over. (Big smile)

It takes time. It takes patience. It takes failure after failure, sometimes, before we're finally willing to see the truth. So stop playing. Get what you need from God. You're already halfway there.

Get to God. He's the only one who can show you what's real real—for real for real.

"Teach me knowledge and good judgment, for I trust your commands." – Psalm 119:66

You're probably reflecting now, aren't you? A swirl of regrets is likely dancing in your mind. You're thinking about that failed business idea, that failed relationship, or all the times you fell short of the goals you set. But, while you're processing those thoughts, let's pause for a moment and dig deeper into the failure to heed correction or discipline—a failure often rooted in pride.

When we refuse to accept correction, we're actually carrying an even heavier burden—pride, stubbornness, or the false belief that we can control everything. But let me tell you something: I am not invincible. And neither are you. We are not God. We cannot control everything. But we can learn. As long as we're still breathing, there's room to grow. It takes humility to accept the truth: if you can't be taught anything, you'll keep failing until you finally learn.

"When pride comes, then comes disgrace, but with humility comes wisdom." – Proverbs 11:2

There is a heavy weight of regret that follows when we discard wisdom—whether it's from our parents, mentors, or even from the scriptures. But here's the good news: there's freedom in discipline. I know what you're thinking: discipline feels like a burden... it feels restricting... But hear me out: being free from the consequences of bad decisions is incredibly liberating! I promise you, there's no feeling like resting peacefully in a king-sized bed, knowing you made the right choice at the end of the day.

Don't add to your load. Whether you're paying attention or not, there's always a caution sign on everything flammable. Life already carries a certain heaviness. You deserve to live a light life. Take off the weight of shame.

As a public figure, there were countless private moments in my life that became public, and most of the time, that was by my own choice. It was always a challenge for me because it made me feel helpless, like I was at the mercy of others. But I had to learn something vital: the focus should not be on what people do to you, but on how you respond to it. You have the power to choose how you react, even in the toughest situations.

The Weight is Over

"Life is ten percent what happens to you and ninety percent how you react to it." – Charles R. Swindell

Like you, I've had people try to tear me down, expose my flaws, or make my struggles the center of their attention. But here's what I've learned: those moments don't define me—they refine me. Those moments made me an author—and now, they're refining you, as you read along. Through it all, I've discovered that my worth is not determined by what others say or how they see me, but by how God sees me. And all I want is to be a great representative of that truth.

The reality is, God has been with me through every public scrutiny, every setback, and every private heartache. There's a freedom that comes with knowing who you truly are. What the world might have used to shame me, God used to elevate me. I'm no longer weighed down by the judgment or opinions of others. And that—my friend—is the real weight loss.

CHAPTER 7:

LONGEVITY LOYALTY

I've noticed a recent trend where some people equate the length of time someone has been in their life with loyalty. Over the years, I've experienced significant changes in the dynamics of my relationships, particularly in how I compartmentalize them. In a modern era where even children now have the right to choose how they live, setting boundaries seems almost foreign—but it is nonetheless crucial.

While longevity can suggest familiarity and shared experiences, it doesn't guarantee that someone is truly committed or supportive. I've had people in my life who were present for many years, yet their actions later revealed a lack of genuine investment. I've encountered so-called "friends" and "business partners" who remained due to convenience or obligation, rather than a heartfelt dedication to my well-being. In contrast, loyalty is defined not by time, but by the quality of the relationship—how someone stands by you in difficult times, supports your dreams, and prioritizes your interests.

For instance, there have been people who were in my life for a short period but showed unwavering loyalty and consistent support. Meanwhile, others who had been around for years did not offer the same level of commitment. Initially, discovering this often led me to instinctively cut people off. But over time, I realized that the depth of connection, trust, and emotional investment is what truly defines loyalty, not just the passage of time.

Values Misalignment: As people grow, their values and priorities often shift. If you find that your core beliefs diverge significantly from someone else's, it might be time to part ways, especially if those differences lead to constant conflict. Meaningful relationships thrive on mutual respect and dedication, regardless of how long they've lasted or how the relational dynamic changes. As your relational equity with someone grows, so does the joy and ease of being with them. These small, consistent investments over time lead to authentic bonds.

Building relational equity is much like building an emergency fund. When starting from zero, it doesn't happen overnight. It's about small, consistent deposits—just like saving a few dollars each month, choosing to eat out less, or making unexpected savings. Over time, these small efforts build up to something meaningful. Building relational equity requires sacrifices, but it results in true, life-giving relationships that point toward wholehearted devotion.

Ideally, both of these elements—building relational equity and reflecting God's love—can happen simultaneously. Be determined to love like Jesus loves. He loves sacrificially, sensitively, sacredly, sincerely, soothingly, secretly, and with a servant spirit. Indeed, the love of the Lord builds relational equity in all who surrender to His heart of affection. The relational equity of Jesus is eternal—unlike the things of this world. God's love is everlasting; He never runs out of compassion for people. Therefore, your devotion to Christ creates unending relational equity.

Many believers struggle to accept the affectionate heart of Jesus, even when it's right in front of them. We are spiritual beings living a natural experience—wrapped in flesh, with eyes, ears, and physical bodies—and often, we are led by what we see, hear, and feel. We succumb to physical urges and mistakenly attribute the lack of relationships to our righteousness, rather than recognizing our failure to make consistent deposits in our relationships. When we honor more than ourselves, we increase the value of our relational equity.

Relational equity is like a checking account, and every relationship begins with a small deposit. What we do with that initial deposit determines how long the relationship will last. Many of us have gone through life opening and closing accounts and maintaining old lines of credit, without realizing it—we just labeled it a relationship. But was it really? Those who believe in Jesus and display His affectionate heart are the only eternal beings we encounter daily, and the relationships with those God has placed in our lives have the potential to last forever.

On my great-grandmother's ninetieth birthday, she invited all her remaining colleagues, friends, and family from around the world to our hometown, Buffalo, New York. We gathered for an elegant evening filled with live music, laughter, dancing, reflection, joy, and celebration. She wouldn't be my grandmother—Constance—if she didn't also invite everyone to her home for an after-party! (laughs) My great-grandmother is sharper than a tack! When the party ended, we honored our matriarch's request and went to "Granny's" house. To our surprise, after receiving gifts from her children, grandchildren, great-grandchildren, and great-great-grandchildren, our grandmother had a gift for us too— as if her life wasn't already a gift in itself!

Having lived nearly an entire century, my great-grandmother, Constance, is a living bridge connecting four generations. Each layer of family—my grandmother, my mother, and I—carries a piece of her legacy, shaped by her experiences and values. On July 31, 2015, when she was eighty-four, I had a ministry assignment on the beautiful island of Oahu, Honolulu, Hawaii. It was a place she had always wanted to visit but never got the chance. Against the better judgment of many, who argued that the trip was too rigorous for a woman her age, she embraced the daring opportunity. What was

The Weight is Over

initially just another assignment turned into the trip of a lifetime when my mother and I made it happen.

I was consumed by an overwhelming sense of gratitude during every meal, every moment, and every memory. Now, at ninety-three, my great-grandmother still refers to that trip to Hawaii as "the trip of a lifetime." Little did she know, she gave me the best gift a great-granddaughter could have—she lived to see it. Talk about longevity! That night, after the party, my grandmother shared that she wanted to give her generations the gift of answers. This was unexpected. My great-grandmother has the rare wisdom to know when to speak and when to stay silent. Her presence is anything but quiet, though one might presume the opposite. For as long as I've known my Granny, she's been a woman of intention, class, and thoughtfulness. She is a listener and a thinker.

"Ask me any question you want, and I will answer it," she said. Question after question filled the air, until one from my cousin stilled the room: "What is the most important lesson you've learned in your life, Granny?" Her answer resonated deeply: "At ninety years old, I've learned that while longevity is a gift from God, it's loyalty—rooted in love and faith—that gives life its true purpose. It's not about balancing the two; it's about knowing which end of the teeter-totter to be on."

That wisdom taught me the importance of investing in those loyal hearts who stand by you through trials and triumphs, for they reflect the love of God. In the end, it is the strength of those relationships that helps us grow.

Finally, it was my turn to ask a question. I asked, "Granny, do you ever stop learning? You've lived ninety years... You were born during the Great Depression... You survived segregation, the smallpox epidemic, and a global pandemic. Do you think there's anything left for you to learn? Some would assume you've learned everything there is to know; many in my generation think that once you reach a certain age, learning stops." She sternly answered, "No. No! You never stop learning, and you never stop growing until the day you die."

Each experience teaches us something new, whether it's about ourselves, others, or the world around us. Longevity in life means witnessing countless moments, but it's loyalty that shapes those moments into something profound. Many people may come and go, but those who stand by you through both trials and joys are gifts from God. Their loyalty is a reminder of His unwavering presence in our lives.

Lamentations 3:22-23:

"The steadfast love of the Lord never ceases; His mercies never come to an end; they are new every morning; great is Your faithfulness."

1 Corinthians 13:4-7:

"Love is patient, love is kind. It does not envy, it does not boast, it is not proud. It does not dishonor others, it is not self-seeking, it is not easily angered, and it keeps no record of wrongs. Love does not delight in evil but rejoices with the truth. It always protects, always trusts, always hopes, always perseveres."

Loyalty, while a beautiful quality in human relationships, is fleeting when compared to the steadfast loyalty of God, which never wavers. In a world where people often disappoint us, we can find comfort in the assurance that God's love and loyalty are always unwavering. Friends may fade away, loved ones may falter, and even family can break your heart. The truth is, as humans, we are flawed. We struggle with our commitments and can easily be swayed by circumstances. We let ourselves down when we unreasonably expect people to love us like God does.

Psalm 146:3-4:

"Do not put your trust in princes, in human beings, who cannot save. When their spirit departs, they return to the ground; on that very day their plans come to nothing."

This verse reminds us that human loyalty, while cherished, is temporary and unreliable.

2 Timothy 2:13:

"If we are faithless, He remains faithful, for He cannot disown Himself."

This profound truth assures us that even when we falter, God remains steadfast. His promises hold true, and His love never fails.

How to love:

Jesus is the ultimate example of loyalty. He stood by His disciples through their doubts and fears. Even in His darkest hour, He prayed for them. His loyalty culminated in the ultimate sacrifice—laying down His life for you and me.

John 15:13:

"Greater love has no one than this: to lay down one's life for one's friends."

This is the true essence of loyalty—selflessness and commitment, demonstrated by Jesus on the cross.

I challenge you now to commit to cultivating a relationship with Him, so that you can reflect His loyalty in your life. To be rooted in Christ is the only conclusive way to remain steadfast when human loyalty fails.

A prayer for tenacity:

Lord, may we always turn to You as our source of hope and strength. In Jesus' name, Amen.

CHAPTER 8:
PERIPHERAL DISTRACTIONS

Fun fact: I am legally blind. I was a squinting seven-year-old in Mr. Quigley's second-grade class at Union East Elementary School when he moved my seat right in front of the room after his frustrating attempts at resizing his writing on the overhead transparency film he would scribble on with dry-erase markers. I've been rocking my nerdy thick glasses or contact lenses ever since (laughs).

My peripheral vision has always been relatively brisk. When I served as the lead teacher at a preschool while pursuing my degree as a dual major in Music Education and Early Childhood Development, I always felt I had "eyes in the back of my head." I started in the infant classroom, where I was famous for my quick hands and agility (laughs)—little ones are easily distracted. Whether it was catching a falling toy or joining in their spontaneous games, I found joy in their energy and curiosity, helping to nurture their first steps into the world of learning.

Having good peripheral awareness was crucial in the classroom of "the terrific twos" (smiling big). It allowed me to anticipate their movements and respond quickly to their needs.

Inherently, my mom had the same instinct. My siblings and I were pranksters who would always attempt to sneak up on her, only to hear her famous words after we asked how she knew we were coming: "I felt you." She would say, smiling big.

Mr. Quigley was one of the best teachers I ever had—not because he changed my seat (laughs), but because that small gesture was just another example of how he always created a link between challenge and opportunity. In response to my need, he gave me an invitation to fully participate in the learning experience. My teacher understood that education is not a one-size-fits-all journey and that sometimes, a little adjustment can lead to greater understanding and confidence. I came into that classroom every day for the next few days, prancing to my new seat with a sense of pride, eagerly awaiting my optometrist appointment (smiling big). As a student, I felt seen and valued. I had a new focus.

Peripheral vision refers to the ability to see objects outside of your direct line of sight. It encompasses the outer edges of your visual field, allowing you to detect movement and perceive your surroundings without directly focusing on them. On the contrary, concentrating too intently on a central object can limit awareness of surrounding stimuli, creating a sort of "tunnel vision."

Now, I know what you're thinking: "I need to have tunnel vision to lose the weight!" My response is, "I see your point!"

(laughs) Additionally, tunnel vision can have both positive and negative effects. On one hand, it allows for deep concentration and can enhance performance in tasks that require intense focus, helping us achieve our specific goals. On the other hand, it may lead to overlooking important details or ignoring broader perspectives, which can result in missed opportunities or increased risks.

Tunnel vision is a phenomenon that can occur in various contexts, from driving to decision-making, where individuals become so concentrated on one aspect that they miss important details or potential hazards. The challenge is that playing with the options often feels like a dangerous catch-22. Balancing focused attention with awareness is key to harnessing the benefits while alleviating the downsides. Poor lighting can make it difficult to see objects in the periphery, and physical barriers, like walls or large objects, can block peripheral vision.

Mental Awareness:

In our fast-paced world, we are constantly surrounded by noise—both literal and figurative—that pulls us away from our purpose. Amidst the vibrant scenery of life's sunlit path, which beams through a lively forest, our everyday tasks and obligations hover over us like thickets. They rustle and poke at us, demanding attention. Though necessary, these distractions can entangle us in a web of busyness, obscuring our view of the horizon where our dreams rest. True success in staying the course will only come when we disregard these peripheral distractions.

In a world filled with constant notifications, endless to-do lists, and competing priorities, it's easy to lose sight of what truly matters. There are many devices the enemy uses to attempt to kill, steal, and destroy your destiny. One of his favorite tools is the ability to lure our focus. In other words, the enemy desires to get you so distracted that you completely lose sight of the predestined plans the Lord has already prepared for you.

Often, we don't fully understand God's tactics—especially when they don't align with the promises He gives. It can be tempting to avoid what lies ahead, but it's crucial to guard your spiritual peripheral vision. Just as a racehorse wears blinkers to block out the distractions of the cheering crowd and rival horses, allowing them to remain focused on the path ahead, you too can filter out the noise of opinions and societal pressures. Your vision becomes a laser beam, fixated on the finish line of your destiny. In this race, the only competitor is your former self.

I remember competing in a gospel singing competition. I never unpacked my suitcase. I never hung my clothes or filled my dressers. I never settled in. I kept thinking I was going home. Some of the singers had been performing for twenty years and were extremely accomplished, while I was an eighteen-year-old fresh out of high school the past summer. I was intimidated when other contestants challenged me to off-line sing-offs. I hated when people told me I was going to win, because I didn't think I had a chance against the other contestants. And, in fact, I didn't. It wasn't until I was on the show that I realized—my true competition wasn't with the other contestants; it was with myself. I was competing against my insecurities, my self-doubts, and my fears.

Kirk repeatedly said that year, "NO FEAR! ALL FAITH!" With every distraction that comes my way, those words still echo in my spirit. With blinders on, you focus on your growth, striving to outrun yesterday's doubts and fears, allowing your spirit to soar as you embrace your unique journey. Though I didn't win the title of "Best of Sunday's," I certainly wasn't Saturday's worst! (Laughs) There was a thrill in crossing the finish line, knowing that the journey was mine, with God holding my hand every step of the way.

If this speaks to you—this is your sign to reclaim the freedom to run your own race, celebrating the victories that come from staying focused on your path.

"Don't be offended, just get in place!" – Lajuan Goodman.

CHAPTER 9:
LEADING WHILE BLEEDING

Once, there was a humble shepherd who dedicated his time to tending a flock of sheep. Among them was a special white sheep, whom he affectionately named "Lumi," for she radiated with the brightness of her white wool, standing out among the others. As autumn approached, the shepherd began preparing for the annual harvest festival, where the finest wool would be displayed.

One fateful day, while tending to his flock, a fierce wolf appeared at the edge of the pasture. In a rush to protect his sheep, the shepherd ran toward the threat, brandishing his staff. In the ensuing struggle, the shepherd suffered a deep gash on his arm, and blood spilled onto the grass—and inadvertently onto Lumi's pristine wool. Despite his injury, the shepherd pressed on, feeling a strong surge of responsibility. He believed that by leading his flock—even while wounded—he could show how much he loved them.

But as the days passed, the shepherd's condition worsened. The pain in his arm became unbearable, the wound became infected, and, tragically, Lumi's wool was tainted by the blood of her protector.

A Personal Reflection: "Dear Diary"

In 2015, I released an album called Dear Diary. The album was born out of journal entries I began writing after releasing my first number-one album on Billboard—Living Out Loud.

July 7, 2014, 8:37 PM CST

Dear Diary,

The real me is shattered beneath this mask... I'm broken, wearing a tattooed smile. The lustful desires of my flesh-infused past haunt me as I write. I'm submerged in endless turmoil... Wondering why people set out to destroy me intentionally. This world is successfully responsible for my internal ruin. I feel like a dead woman walking. I can no longer feel. I'm numb... But the sensation hurts. Ever hit your funny bone? Not so funny, right?

I hurt my ring finger weeks ago. The circulation was cut off for so long that it caused semi-permanent nerve damage. I can't feel it now—but oddly, it hurts.

I'm an upright woman. I'm not perfect, but I try... Daily, I try to treat everyone right. I've given the shoes off my feet and never boasted. I've sent money to help people who weren't even close to me. I've kept secrets I could have shared. I've demonstrated love to both those near and far. I've forgiven the worst of my enemies.

I've sung for God all over the country. I've adopted children and mentored little girls. I've done everything I can to show the love of Jesus Christ for over twenty years. My heart is no longer in my chest. I have no zeal for life, no reason to exist. My mind is an empty room. My thoughts are dark. My soul is hollow.

I've never regretted anything in life—even the things I'm not proud of... Until this very moment. I wish God had never thought of me. I wish He never purposed for me to be here. If this storm takes a turn for the worst, I cannot survive. I am not strong enough mentally, physically, emotionally, or spiritually.

September 8, 2014, 1:11 PM EST

Dear Diary,

Very frustrated. It took a lot for me to embark on the pursuit of happiness today. Just when I thought I had lost everything, I lost my notes. Every last one. Every song, every idea, every quote, every thought... my book. I really lost everything. I have no desire to write this, but it's better than being depressed. I'm not happy in this space of my life... and I haven't been for months. I wish I was. I wish I could find a way to access that escape...

It always amazes me that the person in the comfiest position is often the most uncomfortable. The one receiving indirect adversity feels the direct pressure in the situation. I'll never understand that for the life of me.

December 13, 2014, 1:23 PM EST

Dear Diary,

I'm a mess! Literally... jacked up! I learned something new this week that has me questioning everything I've ever known to be true... and that is, bad things just happen. And there's nothing you can do to avoid it. All this time, I've grown up thinking that things would get easier with The Lord. Jokers lie.

March 12, 2015, 7:24 AM CST

Dear Diary,

Even though I've got a "New School Twang," I thank God for a solid foundation. To be afforded the tremendous platforms God allows me at 22 is no goodness of my talent or ability... Nevertheless, I realize that "I'm Blessed."

Over the past three years, I've faced serious challenges in my faith because the view I was facing didn't always align with the promises God made me. Yet and still, my will said "Yes, Lord"... "I believe." I lost family members, dealt with challenges in my mind, and even went through a season of depression. But the Holy Spirit reminded me, "It will be alright."

Some days, I was so weak, I couldn't even pray for myself. But I'm so grateful that the prayers of the righteous availeth much!!! Just like God healed me at age 6 when I had pneumonia, today, I truly know what "prayer can do." I've got a testimony! And I learned in school that it's plagiarism to take credit for someone else's work, so I know I must cite Jesus; He truly gets "All the Glory."

I'm so glad that I've got a "Safe House" to run to when I'm bewildered. There were moments when I felt so submerged in anxiety that I didn't think I could swim any longer. But God reminded me of His word: "Cast your cares on me because I care for you!" He said, "Don't worry!" I learned to encourage myself in the Lord like David and got bold with the devil, telling him, "I'm not tripping; I'm dropping that because all I need is Jesus!"

I took pride in knowing how big God is in many situations… And in every case, "Only Jesus" reigned supreme. So now, for every Stellar nomination, for my number-one album, for my new label, and for all the times He healed, delivered, and made a way, God, this is "Your Award."

The Burden of Leadership

There is a burden of expectation that comes with leadership—a lot like the cross. It is a victorious cup of agony. Leaders often face immense pressure to project strength and confidence, creating an environment where vulnerability feels unsafe. In many professional settings, there aren't many safe spaces for leaders to express their wounds or struggles. This lack of openness can lead to a sense of isolation. Leaders are frequently expected to have all the answers and remain composed, even in crises. I have often fallen victim to this expectation.

Transparently, it has often discouraged me from admitting when I was struggling. The fear of being perceived as weak or incompetent compelled me to put on a mask, often hiding my true feelings behind what many didn't realize was a facade of confidence. Because the world often equates vulnerability with failure, I walked in fear for years as a leader—worrying about the repercussions of showing my wounds. I battled with thoughts of others losing respect for who I was, based on my translucence.

I maintained a poised exterior but grappled with so many personal and professional challenges. No one knew what was going on at home when I got on stage. No one knew I cried in my room before coming out on stage. No one knew I was in pain as I concealed my struggles.

The Ripple Effect of Unhealed Pain

When we conceal our pain, several significant changes can occur. Our emotional and mental states can significantly influence those around us. When we're struggling, it creates a ripple effect, impacting our family, friends, and colleagues.

Our moods, behaviors, and attitudes can set the tone for our interactions. Most times, we don't realize how they create a collective sense of discomfort. Emotions are inherently contagious. Studies show that feelings such as stress, anxiety, and sadness can spread within groups. When one person is struggling, it creates a negative atmosphere that affects others' moods and behaviors.

Acknowledging our struggles is essential for fostering vulnerability and trust. When we share that we're not okay, it encourages others to do the same. This mutual openness creates a safe space where individuals feel supported and understood, leading to healthier relationships.

Healing and Leadership: A Collective Journey

After years of pouring from what often felt like an empty cup, there weren't enough paper towels to soak up what spilled over into my interactions with others. To minimize the potential of harming relationships and creating cycles of pain, as leaders, we must recognize the ripple effect our pain has.

Ask yourself this: What are you projecting as a result of your unhealed wounds? By actively seeking healing, we break the cycle of pain and prevent our trauma from affecting others. This journey often involves self-reflection, seeking support, and developing healthier ways of coping. Healing fosters empathy, understanding, and connection, enriching the lives of both you and those around you.

In a world where no one wants to ask for help, yet hardly anyone implies care, healing is a collective journey that benefits everyone involved. Healing is not just a personal obligation; it is a gift we give to those we care about. Bless the world and HEAL. The weight is too heavy for you to carry anyway. You deserve to be whole.

CHAPTER 10:

THY STAFF COMFORTS ME

"The thing that was a crutch, God will use to help you lead."

— Alexis Spight

I was always fascinated by the unique collection of canes that my grandfather, whom we affectionately called "Big Daddy," always had. That man could dress. He and my father are the reason I admire a man with a well-tailored suit, good shoes, and a dapper cologne to match to this very day. Something about his canes added even greater authority to the giant of a man he already was. Similarly, a shepherd's staff, typically a long, curved stick, represents guidance and support. When a shepherd leads the flock, the staff helps to correct the sheep along the right path. The other, less pointed, hooked-like end is used to reel in the sheep when it goes astray. Similarly, the wisdom of God guides us, providing a sense of direction and clarity. The staff serves as a source of comfort. We see this in Psalm 23, where David writes, "Your rod and your staff, they comfort me." This highlights the times of danger or uncertainty. This aspect of comfort is vital, as it emphasizes God's renowned responsibility to protect and care for us.

One thing I love about having The Lord as my Shepherd is that He knows me. I tend to wander and am somewhat nomadic. I could not count it all if I tried—the many times God met me right where I was. There's an imbalance today with the use of the rod and staff in leadership. Culturally, the staff represents authority. It is a privilege.

My big brother, Bishop George Wesley Bratcher, said it best: "The Rod is a call and should be used appropriately." Today, authority is often associated with power and privilege. Leaders have often used their authority without a proper balance of compassion or understanding. This approach can lead to environments where fear of correction overshadows the supportive role of the leader, creating a disconnect between leadership and the individuals they are meant to guide. When leaders rely predominantly on the rod—symbolizing correction and discipline—without incorporating the staff's guiding and comforting aspects, it can result in toxic environments. This reliance on authority can stifle creativity, hinder morale, and reduce openness from servant leaders. Often, individuals are left feeling undervalued and apprehensive.

Good leadership is exercised both thoughtfully and intentionally. Discernment is a gift—and a necessary one when determining the time to correct and how to do so in a manner that fosters growth rather than instilling fear. A rod and a staff speak to the comforting and corrective nature of God. God is not only a chastiser but a nurturer. Omitting the nurturing nature of God stops the maturation process for the believer. Leaders must be equipped with both tools to foster an environment that promotes growth and accountability. Similarly, how often do we seek authority only in part? It would be shrewd to suggest that we cannot have one without the other.

So often we forget to unite with the concept of "having our cake and eating it too." We want the comfort but forsake the correction. If we are real with ourselves, we will admit that not everything good for us feels good to us. I have come to understand that it is more important to be effective than it is to be right all the time. When a person knows they will be guided and corrected with love and intention, they are more likely to thrive and take responsibility for their actions.

On a tangent search for validation, support, and connection, I ultimately had to realize that true safety and love are found in The Lord's divine guidance. On a quest for love, I embarked on a journey toward acceptance via various external sources—relationships, achievements, and material possessions—which only led to disappointment and heartache, as these places often fail to provide the security and fulfillment one seeks. Often resulting in a temporary high, but not lasting contentment, the journey led to feelings of emptiness and confusion, intensifying my feelings of isolation and loss. There is a security that cannot be shaken by—

Realizing that the staff of God is the safest place signifies a journey toward understanding true love, leading to greater fulfillment and resilience in life. By anchoring ourselves in this love, we can navigate the complexities of human relationships with a renewed sense of purpose.

"You know how people say, 'You don't need a pat on the back'? Well, I would argue that science supports the idea that it goes against human nature. At our core, humans are social beings who thrive on connection. A simple gesture of acknowledgment, like a pat on the back, reinforces our sense of belonging and worth. It signals that our efforts and contributions are valued, which is essential for emotional well-being.

Many leaders today deem it unrealistic or unnecessary, but recognition serves as a powerful motivator. When people receive affirmation for their hard work, it encourages them to continue putting in effort and striving for excellence. This positive reinforcement can boost productivity, fostering a more committed environment. Conversely, a lack of acknowledgment can contribute to burnout, stress, and low self-esteem.

If we surveyed the majority of people who have experienced hurt within the four walls of the church or suffered at the hands of a ministry leader, I guarantee you they would all agree that the majority of incidents fell under the guise of "a negative culture" that existed unresolved. A culture of love must be evident to justly proclaim your belief in God. True love covers even while confronting your flaws and weaknesses. It may push us to grow in ways that are uncomfortable or unexpected. This is essential for developing deeper connections and understanding ourselves and others better.

CHAPTER 11:

THE JEWEL OF AUTHENTICITY

"You are a diamond! Do you know what diamonds do? They aren't like glitter, they don't just glisten, they don't just sparkle, but diamonds are tough; the more you cut, the more they shine. Life is going to cut you time and time again, but do what diamonds do and shine!"

I used to think my mom only said that because I was "her daughter." Deducing the value of what that meant, I often overlooked how hard in moments like that she tried to shine a light on the value of my rarity.

In a world where people become so common to things of value, it is hard to imagine the rarity of obtaining something precious—something special, something everybody doesn't have. Everything is so accessible. With just one click of a button, you can meet people, gain personal access to a glimpse of a person's life or career, receive information about a source or topic, and even recreate your identity. With just a flight, you can get a new body or even legally change your name to identify as someone else.

The truth of the matter is that, in wisdom and ingenuity, God created man and woman so indestructibly perfect because His design for us was His image. You must embrace your God-given identity—not your identity shaped by the expectations or standards of this world. Romans 12:2 says, "Do not conform to the pattern of this world but be transformed by the renewing of your mind. Then you will be able to test and approve what God's will is—his good, pleasing, and perfect will."

I didn't have a roadmap for this thing. There is no manual on "How to Do Life Perfect," so that means you didn't get one either. There is no rulebook. There is no "how to" or "what to do and what not to do when" pamphlet for navigating this route to purpose. I honestly don't remember many "this is how's" in my early adulthood. It was rather voiced after experiencing a loss that I would "figure it out."

What do I remember? (Laughs) Mm... that would be the reminders. Never forget who you are. Never forget where you have been. Never forget what you have been through. But "never say never!" they threaten. I disagree in this case. Those "never's" were a eutrophic never-land of glue beneath my feet; so thick, it looked like ice... glassed over a sea of possibilities. The enemy was the inner me.

I couldn't see what "they" saw. For whatever reason, people always either loved me or hated me. I was too "this" or too "that." I wanted to feel "normal." I wanted to be able to enjoy life without being held to a higher standard. I hated that part about myself, and later, I really had to accept the fact that I was disrespecting my creator. The one who made me Alexis. I felt convicted reflecting on Paul's words in Romans 9:20-21: "But who are you, a human being, to talk back to God? Shall what is formed say to the one who formed it, 'Why did you make me like this?'"

It would be like if a Picasso somehow came alive and decided to use its ability to speak to tell the world how much it hated how it looked. Imagine that! Picasso's Les Femmes d'Alger (Version O) sold for $179.4 million in 2015. Many smaller works or less famous pieces may range from several thousand to millions of dollars. We are all God's intentional design.

Psalm 139:13-14: "For you created my inmost being; you knit me together in my mother's womb. I praise you because I am fearfully and wonderfully made."

I don't want to make you uncomfortable; that is not the goal of this chapter or this book. Most people would tell you that I normally have a lot to say, but in this moment, I find myself reflecting deeply on the complexities of my experiences. It's important to create a space where we can engage thoughtfully and honestly, allowing for vulnerability without pressure. I hope to share insights that resonate and encourage dialogue, not discomfort.

Over the past thirteen years, interviewers have always asked me the famous question: So, who is Alexis Spight?

Though I never do, I always think, "What do you mean? I am a single black woman over thirty years old with no children, living in America." I know that definition could be extremely limiting, so I mostly digress.

I want to expound on my initial thoughts when asked that question. Every single day, even if a single black woman is at home, she is one of the most endangered species on the planet. I am not a man. I know nothing about being a man. I absolutely love being a woman, but not just any kind of woman—I love that God made me a black woman. I have been a black woman all of my life (laughs), and I love it here! I have a rich Scottish-Choctaw Indian background on my father's side, but the average white person would probably never presume it (laughs), as naturally, their perception would be jaded by stereotypes.

Although I identify as a child of God, regardless, every day I leave my house to enter society, I am a black woman. Black women often face a unique intersection of marginalization that is shaped by both race and gender. This dual burden can result in specific challenges that impact our social, economic, and political experiences. As single Black women, we often face societal stereotypes that can be limiting or damaging. These perceptions might include assumptions about our personal lives, choices, or even our dreams.

Without an expectation for empathy from the rest of the world, many women have challenged these societal narratives, redefining what it means to be fulfilled. Economically, though, Black women are often paid less than our white counterparts and face higher unemployment rates. According to various studies, we earn significantly less than both white men (which is why the pillar in that of a black man is so necessary) and women, contributing to broader economic inequalities. These disparities limit our overall access to resources, opportunities, and financial stability.

I was on tour... Remember, it was 2018 when I collapsed after ministering in Las Vegas, Nevada, and the doctors discovered an eight by five by seven kidney stone on the right side, getting ready to obstruct my ureter. After flying to Mississippi for an emergency procedure during Hurricane Harvey, the doctor successfully completed my surgery, removed my catheter, and I was sent to my hospital room for recovery. Just when one of my spiritual mothers stepped out of the room to get some ice, I started eating my first meal when a woman in normal clothes and a name tag came in asking me questions that were not common.

"You are not Alexis Spight from TV, are you?" she asked, proceeding to take a selfie with me, still only in a hospital gown. I beckoned desperately for her not to take a picture or video of me in such a vulnerable moment, saying, "Please! No! Don't! Please!! DON'T DO THAT! I am not dressed!" The woman insisted, "Girl'll? Whatchu talkin' bout?! I'm gon' get me THIS picture! What are you doing here?"

My affiliates and the other staff investigated the incident only to discover there was no trace of the "liaison's" name in the staff directory. I have absolutely no idea who this woman was, nor how she found me, or what would have happened had she not uncomfortably and awkwardly exited. You may know already, but (in case you didn't), in healthcare, Black women frequently encounter bias.

Maternal mortality rates highlight the urgent need for systemic change; Black women are disproportionately affected by higher rates of complications during childbirth and rigorous surgeries, often due to negligence and racial bias. We see it now in government. For the first time in history, a black woman is running for president of the United States of America, and even Black women themselves wrestle with supporting her. It is the same with corporate leadership. We Black women remain underrepresented. While strides are being made, we face barriers to advancement and recognition. This lack of representation perpetuates redundant policies and practices that do not always address our specific needs or our perspectives.

"You are a strong black woman." That is a good observation of me, some might think. The belief that it is instinctively the nature of a Black woman to be strong is a complex topic, and perspectives on this can vary widely. I personally believe that it is inherent. Some might argue that cultural and societal influences play a significant role in shaping notions of strength. I do not disagree.

Proverbs 31:25: "She is clothed with strength and dignity; she can laugh at the days to come."

This verse speaks to the strength and resilience found in a virtuous woman. It suggests that strength is not exclusively instinctual; it can also be cultivated.

Defining strength can be influenced by cultural narratives. Many women today may feel pressure to embody strength in various forms—emotionally, physically, or socially—due to societal expectations. This can lead to the perception that strength is an inherent trait rather than a response to circumstances.

Luke 1:38 shows Mary's acceptance of her role as the mother of Jesus, despite the potential for societal backlash. There had to be a strength in that, and faith that God would uphold her. Her response exemplifies a deep trust in God's plan, showcasing how spiritual strength can be a huge aspect of a woman's identity. Strength can be situational and may evolve over time, shaped by how we manage life's conflicts.

Did you know that a high-quality diamond may be worth more than an equivalent weight of gold? I explored my mother's

The Weight is Over

decree and discovered that the rarity of a diamond puts it in demand. Diamonds also carry significant weight. They are often associated with huge milestones such as engagements, anniversaries, and other special occasions, which enhances their perceived value.

You are always the perfect invite to everything important. You are a key element. Your presence is valuable. Your presence is always highly requested because you are an atmosphere changer. People know that when they have you in the room, there is a shift.

Did you know that you are worth more than gold? Each of us has a certain amount of melanin pressed between thin layers of our skin. Everyone—black, white, or mixed-race—has tiny bits of protein containing pigment alive and well, nestled in the bottom layer of the skin. While gold holds a steady place in financial markets as a reliable asset, even today, there are not many things in life more valuable than what makes up who we are.

Skin, with its pigment, is currently valued at four hundred forty-five dollars per gram. The pigment in your skin is three hundred ninety-five dollars more valuable than gold, to be exact. You stand out in every crowd without even trying, like a lost soul on the last pew of a storefront church in revival. Shining bright like a star in the night, even your silence captures attention like a Polaroid picture.

"This little light of mine…" is what I always hear my inner child singing when the world tries to crush my spirit. Being a genuine person is such a rarity that it is foreign. A lot of people wouldn't know real if it slapped them in the face. My mother used to say, "…the problem is, you don't believe fat meat is greasy…" If she was really mad, she would add, "…but it really is! Keep playin' and I'ma show yo tail, I ain't playin', now." (Laughs)

Being genuine, much like a diamond, is a valuable trait that has shone brightly in my personal and many of my professional relationships. Embracing authenticity encourages self-acceptance and confidence, allowing us to feel comfortable in the skin God gave us and less concerned about the opinions of others. I know you are grown, but this weight is not about you. Stop hoarding the glory of God in you! Let it be revealed.

Matthew 5:16 says, "Let your light so shine before men, that they may see your good works, and glorify your Father which is in heaven."

God wants to display His radiance through you.

There is a sacred vulnerability in humbly submitting to God and allowing His glory to be seen through your life. Vulnerability isn't easy—not even for giants. Like paper cuts, even the smallest wounds can have a deep impact. But there is no safer place than in the presence of God. There, our vulnerabilities are never mishandled. Ever.

But let's be real—Jesus isn't walking the Earth in the flesh today. So, we're navigating our faith journey through interactions with people... people who are often flawed, broken, and human. That's what makes it so hard sometimes—to expose ourselves to the risk of rejection when all we want is to be seen for the jewel we are.

Why is it that we always have to experience the consequences firsthand? Why doesn't secondhand advice hit as hard as our own pain? I remember when I was locked up in upstate New York, just before my sixteenth birthday. When I got out, my father asked me, "Why do we always have to learn the hard way?"

I thought I could do what everyone else did. Go where everyone else went.

But I was a Rolex in the subway—and didn't even know it.

Even after the TV show, I struggled with that internal war—cognitive dissonance. I wasn't crazy, just like you're not crazy. But sometimes, it's hard to reconcile our beliefs with the reality we're facing. We start resisting the truth when it doesn't match what we want to be real.

The Bible says:

"Trust in the Lord with all thine heart, and lean not unto thine own understanding..." (Proverbs 3:5–6)

"If any of you lack wisdom, let him ask of God..." (James 1:5)

"For the Lord giveth wisdom..." (Proverbs 2:6)

"A man's heart deviseth his way: but the Lord directeth his steps." (Proverbs 16:9)

Despite the misunderstandings or wrongs we experience; God's plan still stands. The old saints used to say, "Be encouraged!" You can't afford to sit in bitterness or betrayal. Keep your eyes on the path God carved out for you. His sovereignty outweighs every setback.

People can't determine your worth—God already did.

1 Peter 2:9 tells us: "You are a chosen generation, a royal priesthood, a holy nation, a peculiar people…" You really are different. Special. And I know this isn't the first time you've heard that, but maybe you needed a reminder.

Like my Bishop says: "A king or queen doesn't come down off the throne for anyone."

Genesis 1:27 says you were made in the image of God. That means you are walking royalty. A living, breathing vessel of divine beauty.

And Psalm 139:14 says: "I will praise thee; for I am fearfully and wonderfully made…"

Being a rare jewel means you automatically stand out.

Be you. Be true.

I know people can't always recognize the real when they see it—but remember: Cubic zirconias can fool almost anybody.

They may look the part, but they lack depth, value, and authenticity.

Not everything that glistens is gold. Not everything that shines is pure.

You might be asking, "So what are you saying, Lex?"

I'm saying this:

You are a precious jewel.

Not everyone can access you—and that's intentional.

Just like a true gem, your worth isn't for everyone to handle. You need discernment in your relationships and in your choices. Because in the wrong hands, even something rare can be mishandled.

I've been there. What I needed was wisdom in my associations and decisions.

So, here's my advice:

Surround yourself with people who see you, honor your value, and protect your peace.

Let God shine through you.

Don't hoard the glory inside you.

Matthew 5:16 reminds us:

"Let your light so shine before men, that they may see your good works, and glorify your Father which is in heaven."

You are light. You are worth more than gold. And your authenticity is your superpower.

Let it shine.

1 Samuel 16:7, one of my favorite scriptures, says:

"For the Lord seethe not as man seethe; for man looked on the outward appearance, but the Lord looked on the heart."

You are who God says you are.

No matter what you're facing — the doctor's report, bad news, tension in your home, financial struggles, job issues, or concerns with your children — you are still worth more than you could ever imagine.

I pastor about eleven middle school boys, and they're always talking to me about a girl they like. I always ask, "Well, what do you like about her?" And without fail, the answer is the same:

"She sooo fine, YP!" (Youth Pastor)

It makes me chuckle every time, but it also reminds me of something deeper. Like children, we all get excited when we see something we like on the outside.

But Proverbs 31:30 reminds us:

"Favour is deceitful, and beauty is vain: but a woman that feareth the Lord, she shall be praised."

I assumed most women would pick up this book due to the algorithm — but if you're a rare gem of a man reading this, know that God gave me this word for you.

(Mothers, if you're reading this, feel free to pass it on to your sons if you're led to.)

Man of God, make sure she's saved.

Make sure she knows Jesus as her personal Lord and Savior.

She'll be an umbrella during the storms of life.

Let her life, not just her looks or words, speak for her.

Matthew 7:16 tells us:

"Ye shall know them by their fruits. Do men gather grapes of thorns, or figs of thistles?"

The Weight is Over

Evaluate character through the fruit of someone's life, not the flash of a moment. It's in the emotional terrains of life where that fruit becomes your support and foundation.

Ask yourself:

Are the outcomes of my life aligned with what I believe?

Where might I be compromising?

Because remember:

"Without faith, it is impossible to please God." — Hebrews 11:6

This is only a test of time.

And as 2 Corinthians 13:5 reminds us:

"Examine yourselves, whether ye be in the faith; prove your own selves. Know ye not your own selves, how that Jesus Christ is in you, except ye be reprobates?"

I was raised with common sense and good manners.

In my house, those were one and the same.

If you said something wildly unintelligent — unless we were joking — somebody would give you the look, and you might get roasted in a good ol' "ribbing session." (laughs)

They don't make days like that anymore — those moments of family, fun, and fellowship.

The Weight is Over

Those virtues are rarities now.

But you — your authenticity — is a jewel.

They don't make them like you anymore.

You are to be cherished.

CHAPTER 12:
ALL IS NOT LOST

"After my grandfather passed, my grandmother kept saying she felt like she was in a fog. But the way her grandchildren stepped up made her feel present in the world...

I thought I was in a fog, but I was really in the favor of God.

I mourn the loss of so many family members that I've lost count.

First, I lost my innocence.

Years later, my innocent twelve-year-old cousin passed from a rare form of bone cancer—one typically found in older white males.

Midway through my twenties, I lost my original idea of what it meant to be a family when my parents ended their twenty-three-year marriage.

My siblings and I gradually scattered to different parts of the world.

After finally regaining financial freedom, I lost all my possessions in a natural disaster.

The record label I was signed to dissolved.

The Weight is Over

I lost my management company.

I lost my lawyer.

Friends told me I was acting "funny" after I got signed, since I could no longer sit on the phone for hours—and they left me on my own.

I've waved goodbye to countless investments: plaques, Keys to Cities, certificates, and governmental recognitions.

Because of betrayal and violation, I've lost a lot of my trust.

I've lost opportunities. And for a while—I had lost my way.

In a sea of losses, how does one stay afloat?

When the waves of life come crashing in heavy, where is the raft of safety?

An epiphany happened when I realized: living is not about counting or focusing on my losses, but rather maximizing all that remains as a result of God's faithfulness through every hardship.

A loss in stability can easily grow into a tsunami of regret.

Looking back over those years, I can honestly say that most of the choices I made wouldn't have happened—if I had just been disciplined.

"If only... if only..."

The Weight is Over

I feel like Stanley Yelnats in the book Holes:

If I could have just listened...

If I had just stayed home that night...

If I had never gotten in that car...

If I had never gone on that show...

If only I spent more time doing this and less of that...

While sorting through piles of loss, I remembered a moment with my fashion-forward godbrother. One day, after "Uncle Troy"—his uncle—commented negatively on his outfit, my godbrother clapped back:

"You wasted all that time locked up and ain't learn nothing' about fashion, huh unc?"

Uncle Troy, who served over a decade in prison, responded with words that are engraved on my heart like a pendant:

"YOU thought my time was wasted—I was PRODUCTIVE! I was locked up, but life was still going on for me."

"The Lord will guide you always; He will satisfy your needs in a sun-scorched land and will strengthen your frame." — Isaiah 58:11

Speed Bumps and Spiritual Lessons

The Weight is Over

I was walking down my street to church the other day—which isn't necessarily out of the ordinary—when, for the first time, I noticed the bright yellow caution signs: "Speed Bumps Ahead."

I'm from New York State, so you should know how I drive (laughs).

We get there—and we don't die.

Who honestly prefers speed bumps?

I'll wait! (As they say in school when the classroom gets too chatty.)

Let's be clear: no one likes that they force you to slow down.

There aren't many options when you're facing a speed bump.

You can either slow down, or risk hurting yourself, your vehicle, your passengers—and everything in your path.

Life's journey is rarely a straight path.

Just like speed bumps on the road, we encounter challenges that jolt us and slow our progress. These moments, while uncomfortable, are often essential for growth.

While pursuing my undergraduate in Early Childhood Development, I learned that children and adolescents often experience physical discomfort as they grow. These pains usually show up in the muscles, joints, and legs—often during the night.

Pain is a reminder that we are alive.

My sister Jada told me a few months ago:

"Pain is a reminder that you are not dead—because if you were dead, you wouldn't feel anything."

Pain—whether physical, emotional, or psychological—is always unwelcome.

But it signals that something is happening within or around us.

It forces us to pay attention. It often propels us to change, adapt, or heal.

In that sense, pain is deeply tied to our awareness—of ourselves and our environment.

Figuratively, the term "growing pains" refers to the discomforts or challenges that come with any type of development—personal, emotional, or even spiritual. These metaphorical pains are often necessary. They're signs that progress is happening, even when it hurts.

The key to winning?

Reliance.

Trust in God.

Believe that His plans for us truly are prosperous and healthy.

This trust reignites the fire trapped in my bones.

I never knew why my great aunt Lavonne wanted me to sing "God Is Trying to Tell You Something" at my Uncle Leroy's funeral until I realized how much she understood in that moment that there are moments in life that will force you to slow down.

Similarly, speed bumps remind us to decrease our pace and pay attention. They make you pause. They force us to evaluate and adjust. Similarly, the trials we face can deepen our understanding and resilience. They teach us patience and reliance on God, guiding us to appreciate the smoother stretches that follow.

I was walking and texting at the same time because there was little to no movement in my quiet neighborhood. While paying no attention, I stumbled over my own foot in an attempt to miss the doggone speed bump! (Laughs)

Family, there is a major difference between speed bumps and roadblocks. Remember, roadblocks cut off the path, causing you to have to reroute your trip, and often cause you to go off track from where you were intended to arrive.

Though inconvenient, the next time you encounter these bumps in the road, remember that they are not roadblocks but growth opportunities. Each challenge shapes you, preparing you for what lies ahead. Embrace them as part of your journey, trusting that God will guide and strengthen you through every moment of difficulty.

Though you feel exhausted and overwhelmed, I challenge you to persevere.

Isaiah 40:29–31

"He gives strength to the weary and increases the power of the weak. Even youths grow tired and weary, and young men stumble and fall, but those who hope in the Lord will renew their strength. They will soar on wings like eagles; they will run and not grow weary; they will walk and not be faint."

Nehemiah 8:10

"Do not grieve, for the joy of the Lord is your strength."

I needed that when I lost my best friend in real life... my grandfather. My BigDaddy.

I will never forget how he would always remark on how he anointed me with oil immediately right after my birth and immediately dedicated me to The Lord.

"I held you and prayed for you for hours... that the Lord would raise you up to be a mightily anointed woman of God."

I am not sure that I will ever be loved like that again... but to have experienced a love like that is inconceivable.

I know that God is real because of that love. An unconditional love that never wavered and was always consistent—only God could love me enough to allow me the experience His life. My grandfather... a human truly after the heart of God.

Loss is an inevitable part of life, but here's the good news: Your loss is not in vain.

Losing a loved one is one of the most profound and painful experiences we can face. The weight of grief can feel overwhelming, and amid such sorrow, it's easy to question the meaning behind the loss.

I can assure you, after losing who deep down I often felt was the only man who loved me without judgment, that God does not waste our pain—even in the darkest of times.

It was right after I lost my grandfather that I was consecrated minister and Youth Pastor shortly following. The torch had been passed.

After the hurricane and the loss of my dog and possessions... after the loss of my record label... after what I felt was the loss of my career, I found myself in the middle of the woods writing in an old truck. I was like Queen Latifah in the movie Last Holiday, asking, "Why, Lord?" (Laughs) True story!

I felt like no one could truly understand what I was going through and how my losses were impacting me.

Hebrews 4:15–16

"For we do not have a high priest who is unable to empathize with our weaknesses, but we have one who has been tempted in every way, just as we are—yet he did not sin. Let us then approach God's throne of grace with confidence, so that we may receive mercy and find grace to help us in our time of need."

Jesus experienced loss, suffering, and grief. When He stood at the tomb of His friend Lazarus, He wept (John 11:35). True friends don't just let you go through alone, but they are hurt by your suffering and sit in your grief with you. I am grateful for the amazing relationships God has blessed me with—those who don't just sympathize, but rather empathize. Jesus is not distant from empathizing with our sorrow; He is with us in our pain. He knows the gut-wrenching pain of loss firsthand. There is grace in that empathy.

Revelation 21:4

"He will wipe every tear from their eyes. There will be no more death or mourning or crying or pain, for the old order of things has passed away."

In Revelation 21:4, God promises a future where there will be no more death, mourning, crying, or pain. There will be new joys, and you are going to live to see them. I release a strength to endure the pain of loss, knowing that one day, there will be no more tears. Life often brings us seasons of sorrow and loss. During these moments, it can feel as though our grief will never end—that the night of pain will stretch on forever. I thought I would never see the sun come up. When I lost my grandfather, the heartache of unmet expectations clouded my mind like the fog above Stone Mountain in the morning. It is so easy to find ourselves in the depths of sorrow, asking, "How long will this pain last?"

Psalms 30:5 says:

"Weeping may endure for a night, but joy comes in the morning."

I remember that red truck in the middle of the woods. I began writing in it as a projection of my frustrations with how overweight I had become. I was carrying so much and felt I had no safe place to unpack. I asked God why I wasn't at the top where He promised, over and over again, and He continued to show me myself. Each time I'd beckon for God to give me an answer to why I felt stuck, He gave me a mirror.

Fun fact: I used to want to be a plastic surgeon. I used to watch Extreme Makeover and Dr. 90210 like crazy. As a painter, sculptor, and designer, I have always admired the human physique. I was fascinated with the art in the process. It had been years since I had even thought about those shows until the whole BBL wave happened.

We're going off the deep end here, but here goes nothing: I support everyone's weight loss journey—mainly because I even considered cosmetic surgery once. Most people say they could not tell, but at five foot three and a half inches tall, I was a little over two hundred pounds at my heaviest weight. My decision to lose the weight naturally came through my willingness to acknowledge that weight loss was mind over matter.

My ex-boyfriend taught me that. Isn't it funny how your past can teach you? God gives us so much mercy that we become encouraged to boldly live out our lives with purpose, withholding no regrets.

Matthew 7:24-27

"Therefore, everyone who hears these words of mine and puts them into practice is like a wise man who built his house on the rock."

Building your hopes on the treasures of this world is like quicksand. The more you strive to possess it, the more it can entrap you. We can get so caught up in the complexities of life that we forget the basics. When life gets heavy, it's often because we've drifted from the simple truths of God's Word and His promises. This world must get back to God, get back to prayer, worship, and actually believe the Bible.

The enemy does not want you to read it because it opposes everything about what he's been trying to convince you regarding this weight.

In this life, time is going to test you. Study every trial to pass the tests. We don't know how much time we have, so we must live intentionally. Students on the honor roll are intentional. Don't just pass the test—keep your faith up and pass with flying colors.

Ephesians 5:15-16

"Be very careful, then, how you live—not as unwise but as wise, making the most of every opportunity, because the days are evil."

Time is a gift, but it's also irrevocable. You cannot get it back. The time is now to step to the other side of fear. The decisions we make today help shape our future. The weight we carry can often be the result of procrastination. God will redeem the time and make every moment count for His glory.

I am not in the middle of the woods anymore, and that's because of the book I started writing in that red truck in the middle of those woods. I didn't know it was a book. The weight of the pain I carried, while still in faith, led to a revelation of God's glory in my life. You know how you watch a movie and it fades to black? Don't forget, movies fade in from black too.

I hear you again, "What are you saying, Spight?" I am saying, remember that every time it gets dark, that does not mean it is the end. This is not your end. You cannot die until you see destiny. Say it with me: If God said He will provide, He will. If He said He will heal, He will. God is not a man that He should lie. Every promise He has made is yes and amen. God has the final say. He will do just what He said He will do if you believe. Prayer is the key, but faith unlocks the door. YOU HAVE COME TOO FAR AND ARE WAY TOO CLOSE TO QUIT!

Galatians 6:9

"Let us not become weary in doing good, for at the proper time we will reap a harvest if we do not give up."

Don't you dare give up. I am counting on you! Your grandmother prayed too many prayers and cried too many tears for you, AND I WORKED TOO HARD ON THIS BOOK! The weight wants you to quit. But start walking. Taking things one day at a time can be overwhelming because of the amount of possibilities within twenty-four hours. My motto is, "One moment at a time... One breath at a time."

I used to be a quitter. Any time I was unhappy, I gave the gift of my absence. But God rewards those who stay faithful. Longevity in our loyalty to God, even when it's hard, is indicative of our faith. The harvest comes to those who do not give up, even when the weight feels unbearable.

The Weight is Over

I was uncomfortable in those waist trainers and body shapers, and I couldn't wear what I wanted to wear at the size I was. I remember the bruises from the duct tape under my clothes when I would forget my corset. It was so tight. But I needed that, I thought. "No waist" so they can say "she's snatched!"— just trying to fit in.

It was on the red carpet after my final interview for the evening at the Stellar Awards one year that I passed out and realized that if I didn't make up my mind, I was going to die trying to be great. I didn't want to be all dressed up with nowhere to go except a casket as a result of premature death due to my neglect of myself.

You cannot afford to be distracted. It was the first day of my commitment to being a pescatarian. I went to my cousin's house to hang out and proudly tell her about my new lifestyle choice. Without realizing it, I grabbed a flat honey mustard wing, fried hard, and started devouring it. Two seconds in, my cousin was hollering with laughter as if Bernie Mac was still alive. With a mouth full of chicken, I said, "What the heck are you laughing about? Did you do something to my food?" Still laughing, she said, "I thought you said you didn't eat meat?!"

Frantically spitting the chicken into my napkin, I felt like I had failed. I thought my journey was over that day. Because I wasn't paying attention, I broke my commitment. Distractions are one of the heaviest weights we carry. They pull us off course and steal our focus from the purpose. The key to lifting that weight is focusing on Jesus and laying aside anything that hinders our progress. Your weaknesses are a platform for power.

The best thing about having Jesus as a Savior is He never leaves us without a testimony. I was detoxing my body, and God was detoxing my life through countless series of perpetual losses. I didn't want to lose weight only to end up right back where I was, so I realized I would have to do the hard work and start forming healthy habits. But first, I needed to look at my life and see what I was hoarding.

A person who had lost everything I could touch, I felt like a bankrupt scoundrel searching for antiques in my dining room to auction for food. I didn't think I had anything to give. But I kept writing because I couldn't just die without living up to my full potential. I had to get out of my own way. One moment at a time. One breath at a time.

I have always been concerned about the needs of everyone else, and the weight of responsibility weighed me down the most. It was from a cold garage with a space heater in November that it dawned on me: the weight of doubt had been lifted. You have the strength not only to manage but to finish. You are safe to unpack now. You are free. You have carried the load long enough. Put your bags down. It is time to soar!

Hebrews 12:1

The Weight is Over

"Wherefore seeing we also are compassed about with so great a cloud of witnesses, let us lay aside every weight, and the sin which doth so easily beset us, and let us run with patience the race that is set before us."

I am not singing "Bag ladyyyyy" these days. God will truly restore and give you back double for your trouble. He will make up for every loss, and everything you thought was a setback will set you up for His glory. God is about to set it off!

If you are reading this book, God wants you to know that you are not too far away from Him. You are not too far outside of His will. You are exactly where God wants you to be. I have come to realize that no matter how hard the enemy tries, he can steal your joy, he can destroy your life, but he can't kill you.

WARNING: IF YOU ARE READING THIS, YOU ARE ALIVE. They can't put brakes on God's next move concerning you because you fought and made it out alive.

Made in the USA
Columbia, SC
18 June 2025

cd36f5ad-c478-4de8-ba61-ea27e460127cR01